MW00581285

The Babylonian Empire

An Enthralling Overview of Babylon and the Babylonians

Free limited time bonus

Stop for a moment. We have a free bonus set up for you. The problem is this: we forget 90% of everything that we read after 7 days. Crazy fact, right? Here's the solution: we've created a printable, 1-page pdf summary for this book that you're reading now. All you have to do to get your free pdf summary is to go to the following website: **https://livetolearn.lpages.co/enthrallinghistory/**

Once you do, it will be intuitive. Enjoy, and thank you!

We forget 90% of everything
that we've read in 7 days...

Get the free printable pdf summary of
the book you've read AND much, much
more... shhhh...

Enter Your Most Frequently Used Email to Get Started

**DOWNLOAD FREE PDF
SUMMARY**

© Enthralling History

Contents

Introduction

Screams pierced the night. Within the gleaming walls of Babylon, the young king Nebuchadnezzar II lay groaning in his palace. His disturbing dream kept him from sleep, but he couldn't remember the dream. Calling his scribes, astrologers, and sorcerers, he demanded, "I must know what it means!"

"Long live the king! Tell us your dream, and we will interpret it for you."

"No!" said Nebuchadnezzar. "*You* tell *me* what I dreamed! If you can't, I'll have you torn into pieces! But if you can tell me my dream and its interpretation, I will shower you with gifts and honor."

The Chaldean astrologers looked at each other in horror. "No king on earth has ever asked such a thing! Only the gods can tell you your dream."

Furious, Nebuchadnezzar ordered the execution of all Babylon's wise scholars, astrologers, and sorcerers. The commander of the king's guard arrived at the house of Belteshazzar, one of the king's advisors, to arrest him. When Belteshazzar heard the king's order, he said, "Don't kill the wise men. Take me to the king, and I will tell him the meaning of his dream."

1

"Is this true?" Nebuchadnezzar asked Belteshazzar. "Can you tell me what I dreamed and interpret it?"

"God in heaven who reveals mysteries has shown you the future," Belteshazzar replied.

"In your vision, you saw a huge, shining statue of a man. The head of this frightening image was gold, its chest and arms were silver, its belly and thighs were bronze, its legs were iron, and its feet a mixture of iron and clay. Suddenly, you saw a massive boulder strike the feet of the statue, smashing them into pieces. The entire image crumbled, but the boulder grew into a magnificent mountain that covered the earth.

"Now, this is the interpretation of your dream. You are the king of kings, the head of gold. After you, an inferior kingdom will arise. Then a third kingdom of bronze will rule the earth. The fourth kingdom of iron will shatter and crush all other kingdoms. This kingdom will then be divided. As the feet of the statue were partly of iron and fired clay, it will be partly strong and partly brittle.

"The boulder that grew into a mountain covering the earth is an unshakable kingdom that will bring all other kingdoms to an end, but it will stand forever. God has told you what will happen in the future."[1]

Nebuchadnezzar nodded. It *was* his dream! He promoted Belteshazzar as ruler over the province of Babylonia and the chief of his scholarly advisors and magicians. Then he reflected on the origins of Babylon and where he would take his kingdom of gold.

While the Babylonian Empire was indisputably a formidable force on the ancient world's stage, it was much more! As a horrific drought gripped the Middle East around 2200 BCE, Semitic nomads swept into Mesopotamia, the land between the Euphrates and Tigris Rivers, seeking pasture for their flocks. They never left.

---

[1] *Daniel 2*, Tanakh: Ketuvim. Jewish Virtual Library, 1997.
https://www.jewishvirtuallibrary.org/the-tanakh-full-text

Instead, these Amorite shepherds settled down, developed Babylon into a stunning city, and conquered the rest of Mesopotamia. That was only part of Babylon's metamorphosis.

After the Hittites sacked Babylon, the Kassites of mysterious origins took possession of Babylon; then, eventually, Babylonia fell under Assyrian control. Finally, the Chaldeans led Babylon into the stunning Neo-Babylonian Empire, with a rule stretching from the Persian Gulf north to Turkey and down along the entire eastern Mediterranean coastline to the Red Sea. The Chaldeans transformed Babylon into a breathtaking city, with massive walls glistening in the sun, covered with blue-glazed bricks and mosaics of dragons, bulls, and lions. A towering ziggurat rose in the city center, near the palace with its brilliant yellow and blue walls.

The Babylonians were ingenious in the sciences and mathematics. They observed the night skies, recording the movement of the planets and cataloging the constellations. They studied the Earth's rotation using mathematical models and predicted lunar and solar eclipses. The Babylonians took mathematics to astonishing heights, understanding square roots, fractions, algebra, trigonometry, and geometry and solving cubic, linear, and quadratic equations. They knew how to measure the diameter and circumference of a circle and calculated pi (π) to a value of 3.125. They used the Pythagorean theorem over a millennium before Pythagoras was born. The Babylonians were a powerhouse of innovation and scientific-mathematical development.

This book will unpack the spectacular history of Babylon and the Babylonians. What civilizations preceded them in Mesopotamia? How did Babylon rise to ascendancy? How did the Babylonian religion and worldview inform their lifestyle and achievements? What was exceptional about their renowned leaders, such as Hammurabi and Nebuchadnezzar II? How did they rise, collapse, and rise again two more times?

This history will unlock the answers to these questions and many more in a thoroughly researched, comprehensive, yet easy-to-understand narrative. Whether you are a history buff or simply curious about the Babylonian Empire, this book will bring the remarkable Babylonians to life, revealing how their story unfolded. You will gain an in-depth understanding of how Babylon left its mark on Mesopotamia's culture and history. And not just Mesopotamia, but the world!

What's the point of reading history? Learning history is fascinating: it's all about change. Examining Babylon's three-time rise and fall is truly an exploration of change. Which enterprising leaders galvanized their people into seemingly-impossible conquests? What events triggered Babylon's three cataclysmic falls? How did collaboration stimulate the explosion of mathematical and scientific knowledge? Understanding the history of change in Babylon helps us analyze how political, economic, and cultural change might happen in our own society.

Chapter 1: The Pre-Babylonian Period

What do the world's first city, first sailboats, and reptilian women statuettes have in common? These were all produced by the Neolithic-age Ubaid culture (5500–3800 BCE) that preceded the Sumerian and Akkadian civilizations. Slightly earlier than the Ubaid culture, the Samarra people settled in central and northern Mesopotamia around 6000 BCE. The Samarra and Ubaid cultures overlapped and shared innovations in pottery and simple irrigation techniques; they traded in alabaster, carnelian, copper, obsidian, and turquoise. About 3,700 years later, the city of Babylon arose approximately where the Ubaid and Samarra cultures once intersected.

The Neolithic Samarra and Ubaid were preliterate, but archaeological evidence sheds light on how these people lived. The earliest people in Mesopotamia were hunter-gatherers, hunting wild herds, harvesting fish and other food from the rivers, and gathering the wild einkorn wheat and uncultivated fruit and vegetables. Eventually, they domesticated goats, sheep, and cattle but continued a nomadic lifestyle. They either lived in tents or with no shelter at all, as nothing resembling houses appeared in the earlier Neolithic-age archaeological digs, only firepits, stone tools, and coarse pottery.

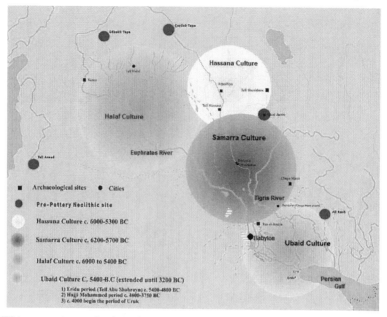

This map shows the location of the Samarra and Ubaid Cultures in the region where Babylon stood about three thousand years later.

Map modified: added labels of cultures, rivers, and the Persian Gulf. Credit: Jolle, CC BY 3.0 https://creativecommons.org/licenses/by/3.0 via Wikimedia Commons; https://commons.wikimedia.org/wiki/File:Mesopotamian_Prehistorical_cultures.jpg

Then, around 6000 BCE, the Samarra culture emerged, with agricultural villages of clay homes; they grew barley, flax, and wheat and herded cattle, goats, and sheep. Their technology included plows, axes, sickles, clay ovens, and grinding stones. Although non-literate, they used one-inch stamp seals with a carved stone picture that left a signature when pressed into clay. They were most famous for their distinctive pottery, featuring a cream slip and reddish designs.

The Ubaid culture appeared about five centuries later than the Samarra in southern Mesopotamia, the region that would later be Sumer. They first lived in reed-thatched homes but later built clay-brick or stone houses and were the original settlers of the ancient cities of Eridu, Ur, and Uruk. Eridu (perhaps the world's oldest city) and Ur once overlooked the Persian Gulf, but over the millennia, the Gulf filled with silt from the Euphrates and Tigris Rivers, and global cooling caused the sea level to lower, leaving these cities stranded in a desert wasteland.

The Ubaid had a relatively sophisticated culture: they used sailboats for fishing and transportation, baked bread in clay-brick ovens, and wove wool and linen. Models of sailboats found in graves provide the first archaeological evidence of this type of water transportation. The Ubaid traded as far south as Bahrain and Oman in the Persian Gulf, perhaps by sailboat, and as far north as Turkey and Armenia. Simple irrigation evolved into a more intricate canal system, feeding from the Euphrates River tributaries and Lake Hammar (freshwater at that time but saline today).[2] This advanced irrigation system required the coordinated labor of a sizeable workforce: a historic turning point.

Like the Samarra, the Ubaid produced distinctive Hadji Muhammed pottery, usually buff but occasionally pink, orange, yellow, or green, with geometric shapes or floral motifs painted in black. Fired at a hot temperature, the pottery was hard and durable. Archaeologists Andrew Moore and Tony Wilkinson discovered kilns in Eridu and Ur in 1990, revealing industrial-scale manufacturing.[3]

Small alien-like figurines of thin women with broad shoulders and reptilian faces discovered in adult graves were even more intriguing. They weren't found in the simple Ubaid temple structures, and whether they had religious meaning is a mystery. Evidence exists of infant skull-binding in Mesopotamia, Turkey,

---

[2] Carrie Hritz, et al., "Revisiting the Sealands: Report of Preliminary Ground Reconnaissance in the Hammar District, Dhi Qar and Basra Governorates, Iraq," *Iraq* 74 (2012): 37–49. http://www.jstor.org/stable/23349778.

[3] A. M. T. Moore, "Pottery Kiln Sites at al 'Ubaid and Eridu," *Iraq* 64 (2002): 69–77. https://doi.org/10.2307/4200519

and Iran to produce elongated heads;[4] however, that wouldn't explain the long, slanted eyes.

The significance of the reptile-woman figurines,
like this one nursing a baby, is unclear.

What happened to the Ubaid culture? A massive flood covered Ur around 3800 BCE, leaving an eleven-foot silt layer. The Ubaid abandoned Eridu about the same time, as global cooling and

---

[4] A. Deams and K. Croucher, "Artificial Cranial Modification in Prehistoric Iran: Evidence from Crania and Figurines," *Iranica Antiqua* 42 (2007):1-21.

increased aridity caused desertification, punishing sandstorms, and freshwater depletion. The Ubaid city of Uruk continued to flourish on the Euphrates' eastern shores and eventually segued into a Sumerian city. Some scholars theorize that the original Sumerians were the remnant of the Ubaid culture.

Whether or not the Sumerians were the Ubaid remnant or their conquerors, they took control of southern Mesopotamia (Sumer) around 4000 BCE. This was when Uruk experienced an explosion of population growth and incredible innovation. They spoke a non-Semitic language isolate, unrelated to any other language, and called themselves the "black-haired people."

After a flood completely submerged Ur, the Sumerians built a city on the ruins of the former Ubaid town. The new Ur grew into a powerful and fabulously wealthy city, as evidenced by the "death pit": the grave of a queen buried with phenomenal treasure and over a hundred attendants who were killed to accompany her into the afterlife. The Sumerians also rebuilt Eridu by 2900 BCE, and the new city featured a palace about the size of a football field.

Kish was another one-time Ubaid settlement that the Sumerians later occupied about 3100 BCE. Located close to the Tigris, east of where Babylon would later rise, Kish was the first city to hold "kingship," or regional dominance, after the Great Flood, according to the *Sumerian King List*.[5] This document, dating back to at least 2100 BCE, chronicled the kings of southern and central Mesopotamia before and after the "flood swept over." The earliest part of the *King List* is probably mythical, but archaeological and literary evidence supports many of the later kings. In addition to Uruk, Ur, Eridu, and Kish, about eight other large city-states sprang up in Sumer.

---

[5] *Sumerian King List*, trans. Jean-Vincent Scheil, Stephen Langdon, and Thorkild Jacobsen. Livius. https://www.livius.org/sources/content/anet/266-the-sumerian-king-list/#Translation

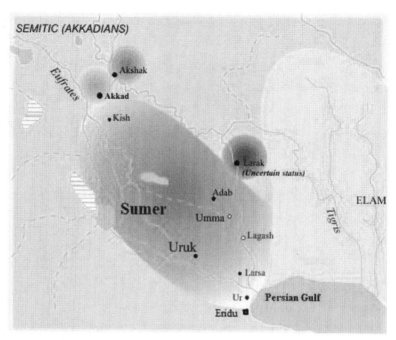

This map shows Sumer's primary cities just before the Akkadian Empire.
Photo modified: zoomed-in, place names added. Credit: Erinthecute, CC BY-SA 4.0
https://creativecommons.org/licenses/by-sa/4.0 via Wikimedia Commons;
https://commons.wikimedia.org/wiki/File:Umma2350.svg

The Sumerians were the first to build thick high walls around their cities to protect them from invaders. A city-state was the walled city itself surrounded by agricultural fields, pastures for herds, and small villages and towns. Each city-state was politically independent of the others and self-contained: able to support its population on what it could locally grow or harvest. Every so often, one city would rise to "kingship," which meant some sort of dominance over the other city-states.

The Sumerians exhibited unprecedented zeal for inventing new things, experiencing incredible breakthroughs in all aspects of civilization. By 3500 BCE, they had developed the world's first writing system, a technique using pictographs (simple drawings) scratched into soft clay, which would harden to form a durable tablet. The pictographs gradually became more stylized into cuneiform, a technique in which the end of a reed was pressed into clay to make wedge-shaped marks. This new written language provided a fascinating insight into the Mesopotamian culture once linguists figured out how to read it! Of course, a writing system required the first schools; it took twelve years to reach a scribe's proficiency level in reading and writing.

The Ubaid and Samarra used basic irrigation, but the Sumerians developed a highly sophisticated canal system for watering their crops and a dike system to control annual flooding. Despite southern Mesopotamia's arid climate, the Sumerians' advanced hydraulic engineering enabled them to produce a surplus of crops, which they could use in trade. Because they depended on the river system rather than rain for their crops, the Sumerians could survive drought conditions. They even thrived through the horrific drought that began around 2200 BCE, which nearly decimated northern Mesopotamia.

The Sumerians were the first to build multistory palaces and massive terraced ziggurats that towered over the city as part of their temple system. By 3300 BCE, they blended copper and tin to make bronze, which enabled them to produce stronger weapons and tools. The royal tomb in Ur displayed the Sumerians' astute knowledge of metallurgy, with stunning silver-plated lyres and gold goblets, daggers, helmets, and headdresses. Their colorful murals and mosaics depicted exceptionally realistic figures.

The Samarra and Ubaid had used stamp seals, but the Sumerians took this a step further by developing cylinder seals. These four-inch stone cylinders had pictures carved on them, so when rolled in damp clay, a picture would emerge, representing its owner's "signature." Hundreds of cylinder seals have survived, and even today, they can be rolled in clay to create an impression. They are invaluable for displaying the level of artistry of that age and revealing aspects of Sumerian history and culture.

This ancient lapis lazuli cylinder seal (left) produced the clay impression (right), a mythical scene of muscular heroes in hand-to-hand combat with a lion and gazelle. On each side is an example of cuneiform writing.
Daderot, CC0, via Wikimedia Commons;
https://commons.wikimedia.org/wiki/File:Cylinder_seal_-
_Oriental_Institute_Museum,_University_of_Chicago_-_DSC07233.JPG

The Sumerians invented the first transportation wheel by 3750 BCE: an ancient seal shows two men pulled in a wheeled cart by a donkey. These earliest wheels were solid wood with a hole in the middle for an axle. Basic carts quickly developed into four-wheeled chariots, pictured in the *Standard of Ur* mosaic around 2600 BCE. A large ass called an onager pulled the chariots, which were cumbersome to steer.

The Sumerians used the sexagesimal counting system, counting by sixty (60, 120, 180, etc.) rather than tens as we do. They could count up to sixty using both hands. They would count the three knuckles of each finger on one hand (excluding the thumb), which took them up to twelve. When they reached twelve, they would hold up one finger of the other hand. Once all four fingers and thumbs were held up, they reached sixty. The Sumerians also developed the sixty-minute hour and sixty-second minute and divided the day and night into twelve hours each.

The year 2334 BCE was a turning point in Mesopotamian history when the Akkadians formed the world's first multinational empire. Who were the Akkadians who led Mesopotamia's Golden Age? They were a Semitic tribe that migrated from the Arabian Peninsula into northern and central Mesopotamia by 2700 BCE, but perhaps centuries earlier: the earliest kings of Kish had Semitic names. They gradually spread into southern Mesopotamia, assimilating the Sumerian culture. Many Sumerians and Akkadians were likely bilingual, and the Akkadians adapted the cuneiform script to their own language.

The Akkadians and Sumerians shared many of the same gods, including the sun god Utu (Akkadian Shamash), the moon god Nanna (Akkadian Sin), and Inanna, the goddess of war and sexuality (Akkadian Ishtar). Later, the Babylonians would worship these gods and others of the traditional Mesopotamian pantheon. Although the Akkadians and Sumerians had different languages and ethnicities, their lifestyles were similar. They lived in flat-roofed, mud-brick homes, and most of the population labored as farmers, herders, or in the construction and maintenance of irrigation systems.

The Akkadians exploded into power under the leadership of Sargon, a man of puzzling and humble origins. Supposedly the son of a priestess who abandoned him as a newborn, a gardener rescued him from the river and raised him as his son in Kish. The king of Kish suddenly and inexplicably elevated Sargon to be his cupbearer but almost immediately began to suspect Sargon of treason and attempted to kill him. Sargon escaped the palace, gathered support, and usurped Kish's throne.

This striking copper sculpture is either Sargon or one of his descendants.

Sargon's next step was to take on the mighty King Lugal-zage-si, who had already conquered all of southern Sumer. With lightning speed, the enterprising Sargon defeated the fearsome Lugal-zage-si and triumphed over Sumer's cities. Sargon then turned to northern Mesopotamia and beyond, extending the world's first empire into Syria, Turkey, Lebanon, Canaan (Israel), and the lands east of the Euphrates and west of the Tigris. Next, he turned southeast to conquer Elam (Iran). The massive swathe of territory conquered by the Akkadians opened up trade routes, pouring fabulous wealth into Agade (the capital of Akkad).

Sargon's younger son Rimush assumed the throne at his death and spent most of his years mercilessly putting down rebellions that had sprung up in Sumer. He flattened cities, killed most of southern Sumer's population, and relocated the remnant to slavery or exile. Rimush reigned only nine years before his own courtiers turned against him, beating him to death with their cylinder seals.

After Rimush's assassination, his older brother Manishtushu ascended the throne and focused on consolidating more foreign lands, bringing the entire Persian Gulf under his power. He also expanded his father's trade routes up the Tigris River to its headwaters in the Taurus Mountains. After reigning for fifteen years, Manishtushu was likewise assassinated by his men, and the throne went to his son, Naram-Sin.

Naram-Sin was a ruthless conqueror who supposedly offended the gods.
Rama, CC BY-SA 2.0 FR https://creativecommons.org/licenses/by-sa/2.0/fr/deed.en via Wikimedia Commons; https://commons.wikimedia.org/wiki/File:Naram-Sin.jpg

Naram-Sin was another brilliant conqueror, like his grandfather Sargon, expanding the empire to its broadest scope. And yet, in popular opinion, his pride brought about the empire's eventual fall. He accepted his people's worship as a god, even building a temple for himself. Not long after, Mesopotamia was struck by the 4.2 kiloyear BP aridification event (2200 to 2000 BCE), with fifty percent less rainfall in an already semi-arid land. Northern Mesopotamia's rain-dependent agriculture couldn't survive, leading to mass starvation and an exodus south to Sumer, where advanced irrigation techniques had enabled the population to endure.[6]

To add insult to injury, the barbarian Gutian tribes from the Zagros Mountains of Elam (Iran) swept into Mesopotamia with guerilla attacks on cities, stripping the fields bare of any produce left by the drought, releasing domestic animals from their pens, and devastating the trade routes. People died of starvation with no one to bury them. The mighty Akkadian Empire fell after only a century and a half of power.

The Akkadian Empire's fall and the population shift from the drought launched Sumer's rise to power again, led by the city of Ur, in what is known as the Neo-Sumerian Empire or the Third Dynasty of Ur. It was short-lived, like the Akkadian Empire, lasting only about a century. It was renowned for its founder, Ur-Nammu, who wrote one of the world's first known law codes. In this era, Ur was also the home of the patriarch Terah, whose son Abraham later migrated to Canaan to establish the Israelite nation.

Utu-hengal, king of Uruk, finally drove the Gutians out of Mesopotamia. Ur-Nammu, who had served as a general under him, rose to power at his death, ushering in Ur's Third Dynasty (2112–2004 BCE). Ur-Nammu defeated a rival king in Lagash and united all Sumer, restoring the Sumerian language, which had almost died out. He built the Great Ziggurat of Ur and numerous other temple complexes. His written law code, preserved until today on cuneiform tablets, dealt with kidnapping, murder, premarital sex, slave rights, sorcery, and more.

---

[6] Harvey Weiss, *Megadrought and Collapse* (New York: Oxford University Press, 2017), 94-183.

Under Ur-Nammu, Ur grew to about sixty-five thousand people, the world's largest city of its day and an important trade center on the Persian Gulf and even with India. After he died, his son Shulgi claimed to have run one hundred miles in one day: from Nippur to Ur. Whether or not that really happened, Shulgi did build a 155-mile-long wall to keep the Amorite herders who had been migrating in since the great drought out of Sumer.

The wall may have kept the Amorites at bay, but the Elamites invaded Sumer from the southwest, going around the wall's eastern end. They sacked Ur and captured Ibbi-Sin, the last king of the Neo-Sumerian dynasty, ending Ur's last dynasty. The Elamites ruled Ur and most of Sumer for the next two decades. Although Ur never again rose to dominate the political scene, it remained a wealthy, strategically-located trade city for another thousand years.

Chapter 2: The First Babylonians

When was Babylon founded? And who first built the city? The establishment of what would one day be the world's largest city is shrouded in mystery. Two curious passages about Sargon the Great and Babylon are found in the *Chronicle of Early Kings* (written around 1500 BCE) and the *Weidner Chronicle* (written around 1800 BCE). The *Chronicle of Early Kings* says this about Sargon in his old age:

> "He dug up the dirt of the pit of Babylon and made a counterpart of Babylon next to Agade. Because [of] the wrong he had done, the great lord Marduk became angry and wiped out his family by famine. From east to west, the subjects rebelled against him, and Marduk afflicted him with insomnia."[7]

---

[7] *Chronicle of Early Kings (ABC 20)*, Livius.
https://www.livius.org/sources/content/mesopotamian-chronicles-content/abc-20-chronicle-of-early-kings

The *Weidner Chronicle* expounded on the same theme of Sargon digging up Babylon (brackets and ellipses indicate damage to the tablet, making it unreadable):

> "Ur-Zababa ordered Sargon, his cupbearer, to change the wine libations of Esagila. Sargon did not change but was careful to offer [...] quickly to Esagila. Marduk, the king of the world, favored him and gave him the rule of the four corners of the world. He took care of Esagila. Everyone who sat on a throne brought his tribute to Babylon. Yet he ignored the command Bêl had given him. He dug soil from its pit, and in front of Akkad he built a city which he named Babylon. Enlil changed the order he had given, and from east to west, people opposed him. He could not sleep. Naram-Sin destroyed the people of Babylon, so twice Marduk summoned the forces of Gutium against him."[8]

Ur-Zababa was the king of Kish, under whom Sargon served as a cupbearer. The Esagila was a temple complex in Babylon, which wasn't built until centuries after Sargon, so that part of the chronicle is incorrect. These two passages make it sound as if Babylon existed even before Sargon became a mighty king (possible, but it would have been a small town) and that its temple complex was already of importance (unlikely). Apparently, Ur-Zababa's command to change the wine libations to the temple was sacrilege, and by refusing to do so, Sargon received the favor of Marduk, god of Babylon (also known as Bêl). However, Marduk was only a minor "city" god of Babylon initially, with no influence over Kish until much later.

Both accounts say Sargon "dug soil" from Babylon's pit, whatever that means, and then built a second Babylon in front of Agade (Akkad), the capital of the Akkadian Empire. Did digging

---

[8] *Weidner Chronicle (ABC 19)*, Livius.
https://www.livius.org/sources/content/mesopotamian-chronicles-content/abc-19-weidner-chronicle

soil imply that Babylon had been demolished? Or did Sargon simply take some of the soil from the sacred city? The meaning is unclear, but somehow, Sargon incurred the wrath of Enlil: the king-making god. Both passages say that Sargon suffered insomnia as a result of his sin.

The *Weidner Chronicle* says that Sargon's grandson Naram-Sin destroyed Babylon's people and received two Gutium invasions as punishment. Babylon was definitely in existence in the Akkadian Empire era, as a cuneiform tablet dating to Sargon's time mentions the city. Also, the year records of Naram-Sin's son Shar-kali-si say that he laid the foundations of the temples of the goddess Annunitum and the god Aba in Babylon in his eleventh year. In those ancient times, the Mesopotamians did not name or number their years; instead, they marked the years by identifying something the king did in that year.

The Babylonians themselves did not seem to have a story regarding Babylon's founding, but the Greeks had several versions of Babylon's establishment on the Euphrates, just south of today's Baghdad. The 5th-century BCE Greek physician Ctesias said Queen Semiramis built Babylon. But Semiramis was an Assyrian queen, reigning from 811 to 806 BCE, over 1,400 years after Babylon was definitely in existence. The Greek historian Hecataeus said Babylon was an Egyptian colony founded by Belos (son of Poseidon and Libya). Abydenus and Diodorus Siculus said Belos built it, but Belos (Belus) was Mesopotamian, not Egyptian.[9] Diodorus even gave a date for Babylon's founding, 2286 BCE, and said Belus ruled there for fifty-five years. His date is plausible, as it would be toward the end of Sargon's reign. The name Belus or Belos is associated with the Babylonian chief god Marduk. However, the word "Bel" or "Baal" in Semitic languages simply means "lord."

---

[9] Menko Vlaardingerbroek, "The Founding of Nineveh and Babylon in Greek Historiography." *Iraq* 66 (2004): 235. https://doi.org/10.2307/4200577

The Hebrew *Torah* said that Nimrod, a descendant of Cush, established his kingdom in Sumer with Babylon, Akkad, Uruk, and Calneh. Then in Assyria, he built Nineveh, Rehoboth Ir, Calah, and Resen.[10] Several scholars believe Nimrod was Sargon the Great, and thus Sargon built Babylon. This would work chronologically and geographically. One Akkadian document listed Babylon as being a border of the land of Akkad (in existence during the Akkadian Empire), and records stated Sargon's great-grandson built temples there.

This figure of an Amorite worshiper is from Mari in Syria, circa 2500 BCE.
Dosseman, CC BY-SA 4.0 https://creativecommons.org/licenses/by-sa/4.0 via Wikimedia Commons; https://commons.wikimedia.org/wiki/File:Damascus _National_Museum_worshipper_from_Amorite_city_of_Mari_5327.jpg

While the Akkadian Empire was in its death throes, Amorite herders speaking a Northwest Semitic dialect surged into central and southern Mesopotamia from Syria, desperate for grassland for their flocks. The Sumerians promptly built a 110-mile wall to keep

---

[10] *Genesis 10:10-12,* Tanakh: Torah, Book of Bereishit.

them out of the south, but the Amorites settled along the Euphrates River delta and made Babylon their home around 1984 BCE. These Amorites worshiped a god of the mountains named Amurru or Belu Sadi. The Sumerians described the Amorites as "the powerful south wind who from the remote past have not known cities."[11]

An ancient Sumerian poem called the *Marriage of Martu* tells the story of a young Amorite man settling in a city named Inab and the discrimination he faced.[12] Martu lived in the city but complained to his parents about the rations for the temple. The single men only had to devote a single ration to the temple, the married men gave a double ration, and the men with children gave a triple ration. However, Martu had to provide a triple ration, despite not having a wife or any children.

Martu decided if he had to pay the temple tax of a married man with children, he might as well be married. He went home to his mother and asked her to find him a wife. His mother told him he needed to choose a wife for himself, but she encouraged him to get married because his wife could help her with all the housework. At that time, Inab had a festival, and Martu and his young single friends went to enjoy the fun.

The god Numucda took part in the festival and brought his beautiful wife Namrat and his beloved daughter Adjar-kidug. As the bronze drums rumbled, the strong champions competed in wrestling matches, and the city was full of onlookers. Martu competed in the wrestling match, and the people of the city kept looking for strong fighters to challenge him, but all the most muscular men fell before Martu. Full of awe, Numucda offered Martu a reward of silver, but Martu turned it down. He offered

---

[11] *Year Names of Ibbi-Suen*, CDLI Wiki, University of Oxford. https://cdli.ox.ac.uk/wiki/doku.php?id=year_names_ibbi-suen
[12] *Marriage of Martu* (The Electronic Text Corpus of Sumerian Literature, Oxford: University of Oxford). https://etcsl.orinst.ox.ac.uk/section1/tr171.htm

jewels, but Martu would not accept them. "I would rather marry your daughter Adjar-kidug."

Numucda told Martu he had to bring milk cows and their calves and ewes with their lambs as a bride price, and then Numucda would give Martu his daughter. But Martu exceeded Numucda's request. He brought golden neck rings for Inab's elders and golden shawls for the old women. He even brought gifts for the slaves. While the marriage negotiations were going on, Adjar-kidug's girlfriend confronted her. Did she really want to marry this uncouth young man? She recounted all the things wrong with Amorite men:

"Their hands are destructive, and they have monkey features. He eats food forbidden by Nanna and shows no reverence. These Amorites are always roaming about; they have confused ideas and only create a disturbance. He's dressed in leather and lives in a tent, exposed to the wind and rain. He doesn't know how to recite prayers or bend the knee. He has no house, and he eats raw flesh! My girlfriend, why do you want to marry Martu?"

But the princess was adamant: "I will marry Martu!"

Ibbi-Sin, the last king of Ur's Third Dynasty, is greeted by a goddess.
Metropolitan Museum of Art, CC0, via Wikimedia Commons;
https://commons.wikimedia.org/wiki/File:Ibbi-Sin_enthroned.jpg

While the Amorites were infiltrating Mesopotamia and becoming more assertive, the Third Dynasty of Ur was beginning to crumble in the south. When the Third Dynasty of Ur was in power, governors appointed by Ur ruled Babylon, and the city paid taxes to Ur. Ibbi-Sin was the last king of Ur's Third Dynasty, and during his reign, the Sumerian cities under his control fell away, leaving only Ur. Then the Elamites attacked, navigating around the eastern end of the Amorite-repelling wall. They captured Ibbi-Sin, hauled him in fetters back to Elam, and ruled Ur for twenty-one years.

In a twist of irony, Ur's rescuers turned out to be the very people they had built a 110-mile wall to keep out. The Dynasty of Isin's Amorite king Ishbi-Erra, who was from Mari in Syria, drove out the Elamites and rebuilt Ur. His son and successor Shu-Ilishu retrieved the stolen image of the moon-god Nanna from Elam, resettling him in his temple in Ur. Shu-Ilishu quickly adopted the Sumerian culture and their gods and even fought more recent Amorite immigrants. He called himself "King of Ur," "King of Sumer and Akkad," and "Beloved of the gods Anu, Enlil, and Nanna."

The high-powered Amorite-Isin dynasty ruled part of Sumer for several generations, while more Amorite immigrants came seeking pasture for their herds. They spread throughout Sumer, maintaining a semi-nomadic herding lifestyle at first but gradually becoming more sedentary. The fifth Isin king, Lipit-Ishtar, wrote a law code over a century before the famous *Code of Hammurabi*.

But misfortune will find you, even if you try to hide! That's what one Isin king discovered, too late, when Isin's astrologers predicted an eclipse, which they thought was an omen that the king would die. King Erra-Immiti put his gardener Enlil-bani on his throne and placed his tiara on his head, hoping that the curse would fall on the gardener instead. However, the omen found the true king while he was hiding out in a corner of the palace eating porridge, and he died. The gardener kept the throne and crown and ruled for twenty-four years, beginning a new dynasty. Enlil-bani, the gardener king, wrote that he removed the heavy yoke from the people, reduced the barley tax, and kept the palace livestock from running amuck in the people's cultivated fields.

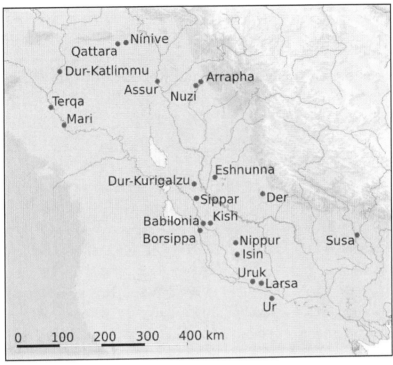

This map shows Mesopotamia's significant cities during Babylon's earliest years.
Rowanwindwhistler, GFDL http://www.gnu.org/copyleft/fdl.html via Wikimedia Commons; https://commons.wikimedia.org/wiki/ File:Mesopotamia_en_el_segundo_milenio-es.svgb

By the time the gardener king was ruling Isin, the town of Babylon, called Babil by the Sumerians and Bab-ilim in Akkadian, was rising to prominence. In 1897 BCE, many of the Amorites came under the leadership of a dynamic tribal leader named Sumu-Abum (Su-abu), considered the first king of Babylon's First Dynasty. Sumu-Abum conquered Kish, Dilbat, and Elip, began the construction of a wall around Babylon, and erected temples. He also built walls for his new cities of Kish and Dilbat. Sumu-Abum worshiped a local god named Marduk or Amar, the god of thunderstorms who would become the god of domination, power, sex, and war. Marduk replaced the Sumerian god Enlil as the chief Amorite deity.

An intriguing letter written to Sumu-Abum refers to a journey of Ishtar (Annunitum) to visit Marduk's temple in Babylon. The writer wanted to carry the goddess' statue to Babylon so that Ishtar could consult with Marduk on a particular matter. The writer asked Sumu-Abum's permission to bring the goddess' statue, saying he would set off as soon as he heard from the king. He also mentioned he was concerned for the goddess' temper during the journey (Ishtar was known as a hothead). [13]

Sumu-Abum freed the Babylonians from the overlordship of Kazallu (Kassala) on the Euphrates River, which had experienced horrific history in the Akkadian Empire. Kassala had rebelled, and Sargon the Great marched to meet the insurgents. Sargon was merciless, flattening the city and even cutting down all the trees, so there was no place "for a bird to rest." When Sargon's son Rimush was king, Kassala's citizens rebuilt their city but then dared to challenge Rimush. Rimush was inhumanly cruel, killing twelve thousand Kassala citizens, enslaving five thousand, and leveling the city to the ground once again. The irrepressible people of Kassala had rebuilt their city a third time, holding the upper hand in the region until Sumu-Abum became the leader of Babylon.

Sumu-Abum's conquest of Kassala appears to be a joint effort of Babylon and Isin, as records of Erra-Immiti, the ill-omened king of Isin who died eating porridge, says he conquered Kassala at approximately the same time. Sumu-Abum triumphantly overpowered Kassala, but the city of Kish, which he had conquered, rose in rebellion, and its leader Manana forced Sumu-Abum into exile.

---

[13] Rients de Boer, "Beginnings of Old Babylonian Babylon: Sumu-Abum and Sumu-La-El," Free University of Amsterdam, American Schools of Oriental Research, 62. https://www.jstor.org/journal/jcunestud

This bust is probably an earlier Amorite king before Hammurabi.
Serge Ottaviani, CC BY-SA 3.0 https://creativecommons.org/licenses/by-sa/3.0 via Wikimedia Commons; https://commons.wikimedia.org/wiki/File:Royal_portrait_-_Hamurabi_-_King_of_Babylon_-1900_before_JC_-.JPG

Sumu-Abum's vigorous successor, Sumu-la-El, ruled from 1880 to 1845 BCE. He had served as a lieutenant under Sumu-Abum and was likely his son. He sacked Kish and Kassala (again) and brought other Amorite chieftains under his command. He built defensive fortresses around the Babylonian region, completed the great city wall around Babylon his father had started, and gained temporary control of Nippur. He dug an irrigation canal called Utu-hegal and built or deepened several other canals. He erected a temple to Adad and a magnificent throne for Marduk overlaid with silver and gold.

Sumu-la-El had a rugged ally in Uruk, whose kings had Amorite names in this era. One of his daughters, Sallurtum, married Sîn-kāšid of Uruk, "King of the Amnānum" (an Amorite tribe).[14] Sumu-

---

[14] de Boer, "Beginnings of Old Babylonian Babylon," 67-8.

la-El consolidated the northern Babylonian cities into one unified Amorite state that presented an intimidating challenge to kingdoms like Larsa or Eshnunna. He replaced the local kings with Amorite leaders loyal to him. Sumu-la-El led the "Amorite Assembly" of tribal elders loyal to him, who considered him their chieftain.

Sumu-la-El's son Sabum ruled Babylon for at least fourteen years. He was the first to build the Esagila temple to Marduk, which housed the statue of the god surrounded by idols of the cities that had fallen to Babylon. The Esagila, the "house that rises its head," was the paramount temple complex in a city considered sacred to all Babylonians, even all of Mesopotamia. He was succeeded by Apil-Sin, who ruled for seventeen years.

The industrious Apil-Sin erected a magnificent new wall for Babylon, gleaming with brilliant blue lapis lazuli stones. Like his predecessors, he dug new irrigation canals and enhanced the ones already there. After the great drought that destroyed the Akkadian Empire, the Babylonians realized the urgency of having an excellent irrigation system. Apil-Sin constructed a stupendous temple to Inanna (Ishtar) in Babylon and built or restored other temples in the city.

Apil-sin's aggressive son Sin-muballit served nineteen years as king, contending triumphantly against Larsa and taking the city of Isin captive. He relentlessly extended Babylonia's borders by vanquishing (or holding) Borsippa, Dilbat, Kassala, Kish, and Sippar. He grew in power, building up the towns and cities of south-central Mesopotamia, which had come under Babylon's rule; however, he fell ill and abdicated his throne to his famous son Hammurabi.

Most kings never see their son's accomplishments, but Sin-muballit lived through part of his son's reign. Did he live to see Hammurabi unite almost all Mesopotamia under his authority? Did he have any recommendations for his son's law code? Did he ever envision his son would be esteemed as a model ruler throughout

Middle Eastern history? If he lived long enough to see just a fraction of his son's achievements, Sin-Muballit must have been extraordinarily proud.

Chapter 3: The Rise of Babylon

Revered as a god in his lifetime, the exceptional conqueror and lawgiver Hammurabi elevated the modest city-state of Babylonia to astounding heights. When he ascended the throne in 1792 BCE (middle chronology), Babylon lay surrounded by four fierce kingdoms that threatened its very existence. Ancient Elam to the east, a prosperous and vigorous two-thousand-year-old kingdom located in present-day Iran, had overrun southern Sumer. Assyria, to the north, was building an immense empire that encompassed Syria, Lebanon, and Canaan and was pressing into central Mesopotamia. The ancient Sumerian city-state of Larsa guarded the southern river delta, and the Sumerian-Akkadian city-state of Eshnunna on Babylonia's northwest border controlled the upper Tigris River.

Hammurabi's father, Sin-Muballit, had already begun expanding Babylonia, bringing Kish, Sippar, and Borsippa under Babylonian jurisdiction. Hammurabi would have been relatively young when he ascended the throne, perhaps a teenager, as he ruled for forty-three years. Following in his ambitious father's footsteps, Hammurabi advanced and expanded Babylon into a thriving kingdom that swallowed up the competing kingdoms, transforming Babylon into the master of Mesopotamia.

As the sixth Amorite king to rule Babylon, Hammurabi's extraordinary reign metamorphized Babylon into one of the most dynamic and influential kingdoms in the Middle East. His first challenge arose when the Elamites of the Zagros Mountains poured into central Mesopotamia, trouncing Babylon's neighbor Eshnunna and savagely enveloping other cities under their dominion.

This figurine of an Amorite worshipper of Amurru is from Larsa.
https://commons.wikimedia.org/wiki/File:Worshipper_Larsa_Louvre_AO15704.jpg

The Elamites attempted to destabilize the region further by instigating conflict between Babylon and Larsa. Hammurabi instead allied with Larsa, and the two cities vowed to fight Elam together. However, when the time came to go to war, the Babylonians contributed the lion's share of military men, while Larsa's king held back. Although he thrashed the Elamites without much support from Larsa, Hammurabi was annoyed by Larsa's reluctance to fight.

Once he drove out the Elamites from Mesopotamia, Hammurabi subjugated Larsa by damming the Euphrates, then suddenly releasing it, covering Larsa with an epic flood. Victory over Larsa gave him mastery over Sumer, including Ur, Uruk, Isin, and Eridu, while he already held Kish, Sippar, and other Sumerian cities as his father's legacy. His triumph spelled the end of the Sumerians' sovereignty in southern Mesopotamia. The Akkadian kings had decimated the Sumerian population, but Sumer had risen to strength in the Third Dynasty of Ur. But now, the Elamite invasion and the Amorite takeover brought this revolutionary civilization to its knees. Its spoken language died out, except in religious, ceremonial, and scientific contexts.

Hammurabi had joined forces with his ancestral Amorite relatives in Syria, the Mari and Yamhad dynasties; together, they crushed Elam and annexed Sumer. However, the Mari treacherously formed a coalition army with Eshnunna against Babylon, attempting to restrict Babylon's power in the north. The attempt failed: Eshnunna fell to Hammurabi's forces, and then the Tigris River flooded, covering the city.

Once he overpowered Eshnunna, Hammurabi took his revenge against Mari. Although the people were his ancient kinsmen, he not only conquered the city but utterly obliterated it. He usually spared most of his conquered cities and even improved them once he held control, but he flattened Mari. Perhaps it was outrage at their betrayal, or he didn't want the luxurious Mari to outshine Babylon.

Next, Hammurabi turned his attention toward Assyria. Like the Akkadians and the Amorites, the Semitic-speaking Assyrians were once pastoral herders, living in tents in northern Mesopotamia but eventually becoming city-dwellers. They had fallen under Akkadian rule; when that empire crumbled, the independent Old Assyrian Empire rose to dominance in northern Mesopotamia under the powerful King Puzur-Ashur I. The usurper Shamshi-Adad expanded the Assyrian territory into northern Mesopotamia and part of today's Turkey. His son Ishme-Dagan engaged in a protracted war with Babylonia.

Although Assyria and Babylon fiercely vied for the upper hand, Hammurabi finally triumphed. He dethroned Ishme-Dagan and forced his successor Mut-Ashkur to acknowledge Babylon's overlordship; Hammurabi allowed Mut-Ashkur to rule Assyria as a vassal king as long as he faithfully paid tribute to Babylon. Hammurabi extended his rule north into Anatolia (Turkey) and west into most of the Levant (Syria, Lebanon, and Canaan). Unlike the Akkadians, once Hammurabi initially conquered all of Mesopotamia, he maintained his control, with no significant uprisings in his lifetime.

With Mesopotamia and even part of Anatolia and the Levant conquered, Hammurabi turned to the west. The Elamites, Lullubi, and Gutians of Iran's Zagros Mountains had been persistent threats to Mesopotamia for over a century, and now the Kassites were also rising as a menacing power in the west. Hammurabi invaded Iran, subduing all of the problematic tribes.

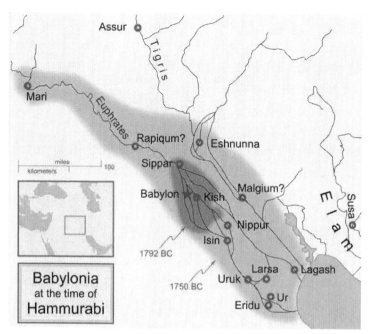

The star shows the location of Babylon. The dark shading is where the region of Babylonia was, and the light shading is the extent of the Babylonian Empire under Hammurabi, stretching from the Persian Gulf up through Syria.

Although Hammurabi was a forceful conqueror, he seemed genuinely concerned for the welfare of his realm's people, with the notable exception of Mari. He was fortunate to begin his reign in a relatively peaceful era so he could focus on ambitious building projects, transforming Babylon into a dazzling city with a well-ordered, streamlined bureaucracy and strong central government.

He raised the city's walls to even higher heights and enlarged and beautified the temples. Hammurabi was a thoroughly involved leader, personally supervising flood management, changing a problematic calendar, and even overseeing the care of the city's massive livestock herds. A vast collection of his letters and administrative accounts have survived on clay tablets and portray a king engrossed in building canals, ensuring efficient food distribution, engaged in beautification projects, constructing public buildings, and fighting wars.

Hammurabi was a micromanager, but he seemed laser-focused on providing for his people's needs and ensuring justice for all. His law code illustrated his concern for ordinary people and his desire for everyone to be treated fairly and decently. Mesopotamian rulers often referred to themselves as shepherds, reflecting their pastoral roots and a desire to provide for the welfare and safety of those under their control. Although several law codes preceded Hammurabi's, his laws excelled for being so clearly written and extensive: almost three hundred laws covering varied aspects of life.

Hammurabi repeatedly formed alliances to fight formidable foes, then abruptly broke them once the danger was past and turned against his former allies. He united with Larsa against Elam, but once he defeated Elam, he formed alliances with Nippur and Lagash against Larsa and later betrayed Nippur and Lagash. He allied with his ancestral kin, Mari and Yamhad, in Syria, and once they'd helped him, he swiftly turned on them and conquered them (although Mari backstabbed him first). It never seemed to occur to the people of any of these city-states not to trust Hammurabi. Ironically, the man known for defending justice with his law code was unjust in the art of war.

Of all the Mesopotamian kings of the second millennium, Hammurabi stands out for being honored as a deity even while alive. The title *Hammurabi-ili* meant "Hammurabi is my god" and was commonly used to honor him. His subjects remembered him for being a victorious conqueror, maintaining peace in his massive kingdom, and promoting justice for all citizens.

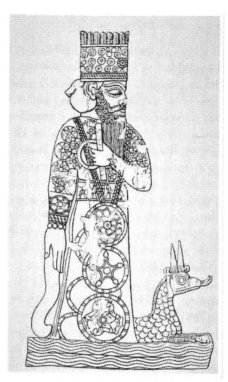

This image of the god Marduk is from an ancient cylinder seal.
https://commons.wikimedia.org/wiki/File:Marduk_and_pet.jpg

Hammurabi promoted the worship of Babylon's city god Marduk on a much grander scale, placing him at the head of the Mesopotamian pantheon of gods. Among his incentives for conquering vast territories was spreading the worship of Marduk; he considered his campaigns against other city-states to be a holy war: spreading the knowledge of Marduk, subduing evil, and bringing civilization to all people. A victory stele that Hammurabi installed in Ur declared:

> "The people of Elam, Gutium, Subartu, and Tukrish, whose mountains are distant and whose languages are obscure, I placed into Marduk's hand. I myself continued to put straight their confused minds."[15]

---

[15] Marc Van De Mieroop, *King Hammurabi of Babylon: A Biography* (Hoboken: Blackwell Publishing, 2005), 126-7.

Like his father, Hammurabi fell ill and could not continue with all the minutia of ruling an empire. However, given that he reigned for forty-two years, he must have been in his sixties or seventies. He increasingly delegated administrative affairs to his son Samsu-iluna, and in the last year of his life, his son was the de facto king. In less than a year after Hammurabi's death in 1750 BCE, the great empire he had built began to crumble.

Hammurabi's son Samsu-iluna ruled for thirty-eight years, but his reign was marked by the loss of control over Assyria and Elam and rebellions in other previously-conquered territories. Nine years into his reign, Larsa led a massive uprising of twenty-six cities, including Eshnunna, Isin, Ur, and Uruk. Samsu-iluna experienced immediate success against the coalition forces when he led a shattering campaign against Eshnunna and executed its King Iluni. Samsu-iluna energetically fought the rest of the rebels for four years, conquering Ur, Uruk, Isin, and finally Larsa in rapid succession, pulling down the defensive walls and sacking the cities. His triumphs ended the Sumerian rebellion temporarily.

However, the far south of Sumer wasn't ready to concede. The province of Sealand was in the marshlands of southernmost Mesopotamia, where the Tigris and Euphrates had dumped enough silt that the coastline extended out into the Persian Gulf for miles past its original shoreline. The Akkadian-speaking people of Sealand, led by Ilum-ma-ili, who claimed descent from Isin's last king, were the next to break free of the Old Babylonian Empire, forming the First Sealand Dynasty. Samsu-iluna unsuccessfully fought against the rebels, who held ascendancy in Sumer for three centuries.

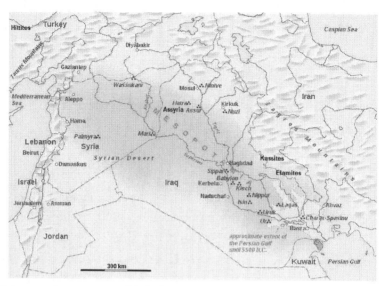

This map shows some of Babylon's rival kingdoms: the Hittites, Kassites, Elamites, and Assyrians. Map modified: names of rival kingdoms added.
https://commons.wikimedia.org/wiki/File:N-Mesopotamia_and_Syria_english.svg

Twenty years into Samsu-iluna's reign, Eshnunna rebelled again, but the king triumphed once more. However, Elam and Assyria both took advantage of the chaos in Sumer. Samsu-iluna had torn down Uruk's walls, leaving the city defenseless. The Elamite king Kuturnahunte I sacked Uruk, stealing precious artifacts, including Inanna's idol; it would take over one thousand years before the statue was returned.

Next, Assyria's vice-regent, Puzar-Sin, staged a coup in Assyria, banishing its Amorite king Asinum, a vassal king to Babylonia. In the chaos, the Assyrian Ashur-dugal stole Assyria's throne, but this led to a revolution by the Assyrians against the usurper, who was a "son of a nobody, who had no title to the throne,"[16] according to the *Assyrian King List*. During his brief reign of six years, six other "sons of nobodies" also reigned, apparently fragmenting Assyria into six regions led by usurpers. No one in Assyria was paying the

---

[16] *Assyrian King List*, Livius. https://www.livius.org/sources/content/anet/564-566-the-assyrian-king-list

requisite tribute to Babylon throughout the unrest, and Samsu-iluna seemed helpless to do anything.

In addition to losing large sections of the empire, Samsu-iluna had to confront new enemies. Sutean tribes from the Mediterranean were staging slave raids in the cities of Idamara and Arrapha in the northeast, compelling Samsu-iluna to pass a law forbidding Babylonians from buying enslaved people captured from Babylonian territories. In his ninth year, while simultaneously fighting the Sumerian coalition, the Kassites invaded: the first mention of this tribe in historical accounts. Of mysterious origins, the Kassites would successfully seize power 170 years later and rule Babylon for four centuries. But for now, Samsu-iluna managed to repel them.

Samsu-iluna also went on the offensive against Amorite tribes not aligned with Babylonia and annexed their territories. He killed the king of Apum in northeastern Syria and demolished the city, and in the following year, he campaigned successfully against Terqa, which was close to Mari. In his thirty-fifth year as king, Samsu-iluna was put on the defensive when he successfully ejected a coalition army of Amorites invading from Syria.

By the end of Samsu-iluna's reign, Babylonia had shrunk down to almost where it was before Hammurabi became king. He did retain control over the vital trade on the Euphrates River as far northwest as Mari. Another thing Babylon retained was its sacred status. Hammurabi had named Babylonia a "holy city," making it Mesopotamia's sacred city instead of Nippur. Despite all the loss of land, Babylonia maintained its reputation as a sacred destination.

In addition to defending Babylonia against internal revolutions and external invasions, Samsu-iluna instituted the Babylonian calendar based on a previous Sumerian calendar from the Third Dynasty of Ur. The calendar had twelve lunar months, plus an extra month to be inserted as needed. Every seventh day was a "holy day," during which citizens had to refrain from certain activities.

Samsu-iluna's son Abi-Eshuh ruled Babylonia next for twenty-eight years. He successfully repelled a second Kassite invasion in his fourth year as king, unsuccessfully attempted to capture the Sealand ruler by damming the Tigris River, and failed to repel Elamite invasions into Babylonia under King Kutir-nahhunte I. In their raids of thirty Babylonian cities, the Elamites stole the enormous diorite stone on which Hammurabi's law code was carved. They hauled it back to Susa, where it remained for over three thousand years until finally discovered in archaeological digs in 1901.

Abi-Eshuh's son Ammi-Ditana and grandson Ammisaduqa were the subsequent two Babylonian kings, blessed with long and peaceful reigns, with no war or invasions recorded. Babylonian scholars compiled the *Venus Tablet of Ammisaduqa* during King Ammisaduqa's reign: careful records of the planet Venus' risings and settings, with other astronomical observations such as eclipses.

King Samsu-Ditana then reigned as Babylon's last Amorite king. The Hittites dashed his hopes of enjoying the peaceful reigns of his father and grandfather; however, his own actions contributed to Babylonia's fall. Rather than maintaining a substantial standing army, he had permitted able-bodied men to make payments for not serving in the military.

The Hittite kingdom of Hatti lay in the far northwest, between the Mediterranean and the Black Sea. Led by King Mursili I, the Hittites first invaded Aleppo (in Syria) and brought back captives. King Mursili then marched into Mesopotamia's heartland, sacking Babylon and carrying away captives and booty, but leaving the shattered city abandoned. The Babylonians carefully noted and recorded omens, such as lunar and solar eclipses, which they believed foretold the death of a king. In this case, their superstition proved correct. Twin eclipses, first a lunar and then a solar eclipse, occurred within two weeks of each other, just before the Hittites attacked.[17]

Why did the Hittites invade from so far away and then just leave? One theory is that a massive volcanic eruption on the island of Thera disrupted weather patterns and the wheat harvests in the Hittite homeland. The Hittites might have been raiding a distant land for wheat.[18]

Perhaps most devastating of all for the remnant of Babylonian civilization was that the Hittites stole the image of the god Marduk. Marduk was Babylon's patron god, but Hammurabi had also been promoting him as the new leader of the Mesopotamian pantheon. People made pilgrimages to Babylon from all over Mesopotamia just to worship Marduk in the sacred city and seek omens from him. The ancient Mesopotamians believed the god inhabited his image. How could Babylon ever hope to revive without Marduk? What no one knew at the time was that this was just one of many journeys Marduk would take as his image was stolen, returned, and stolen again. An epic poem was even written about Marduk's wanderings from his own perspective.

The Hittite invasion left the city mostly uninhabited, ending the Amorite political reign in Mesopotamia forever. It also spelled the end of the Amorites in Mesopotamia as a distinct ethnic group, and within four hundred years, the Amorites disappeared from history altogether. However, Hammurabi's influence lived on through his example as a leader and through his law code, which the succeeding Kassite Dynasty adopted, and which influenced other Middle Eastern laws.

---

[17] Peter J. Huber, *Astronomical Dating of Babylon I and Ur III.* (Cambridge: Harvard University, 1982).
[18] William J. Broad, "It Swallowed a Civilization," *New York Times*, October 21, 2003. https://www.nytimes.com/2003/10/21/science/it-swallowed-a-civilization.html

In a hymn apparently written by Hammurabi, he extolls himself:

"I am the king, the brace that grasps wrongdoers, which makes people of one mind,

I am the great dragon among kings who throws their counsel in disarray

I am the net that is stretched over the enemy,

I am the fear-inspiring, who, when lifting his fierce eyes, gives the disobedient the death sentence,

I am the great net that covers evil intent,

I am the young lion, who breaks nets and scepters,

I am the battle net that catches him who offends me.

I am Hammurabi, the king of justice."[19]

---

[19] Van De Mieroop, *King Hammurabi of Babylon,* 127.

Chapter 4: The Kassite Dynasty

"Fallen, fallen is Babylon! All the images of her gods lie shattered on the ground!"[20]

For twenty-five years, Babylon was a ghost town. The Hittites had hauled off the grain stores, temple treasures, and thousands of captives. They had leveled nearly all the buildings, and most survivors fled. Perhaps a few straggled back from where they had hidden and huddled in the few remaining structures. Possibly they gleaned a small harvest from the remnants left in the fields and rounded up some of the stray goats and sheep. They may have been able to plant a few fields and live off the proceeds.

And then, after twenty-five years, the Kassites marched into town and assumed residence in the abandoned city. Twice they had tried to take possession of Babylon: during the reigns of Hammurabi's son Samsu-iluna and grandson Abi-Eshuh. Both times, the Babylonians had repelled the Kassites. But now, Babylon had no king and just a minuscule population struggling to survive.

---

[20] *Isaiah 21:1,* Tanakh: Navi: The Book of Yeshayahu.

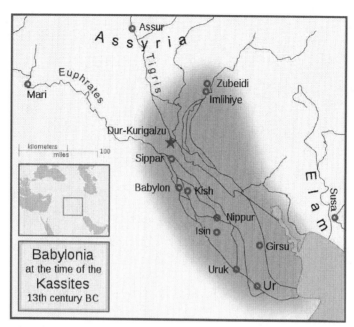

Babylonia's territory during the Kassite rule stretched from the Persian Gulf to the border of Assyria.

Who were the Kassites, and from where did they come? They may have come from the Zagros Mountains of Iran, but even that is uncertain, based on where they fled when they were eventually driven out of Babylon centuries later. They spoke a non-Semitic language isolate, unrelated to the languages of the Elamites, Gutians, or other Iranian people. They were not mentioned in any Middle Eastern histories before their failed attacks on Babylon.

If they were from the Zagros Mountains, they must have only lived there for two or three centuries. They were never mentioned during the many military campaigns the Akkadian Empire waged in the region. They may have had an Indo-European heritage or lived near Indo-Europeans, as their gods were similar to the Vedic pantheon (the ancestors of the Hindu gods and Zoroastrian demi-gods).

Kassite names began to pop up in the city of Larsa during Hammurabi's reign, and records with names of Kassite people indicated they infiltrated Babylonia during the reigns of Hammurabi's descendants. They appeared to have served as military mercenaries for the Babylonians and were known for breeding horses and manufacturing swift war chariots. While the Kassite direct invasions failed, Kassites slowly worked their way into Babylonian society.

Some scholars suggest that the Kassites were in alliance with the Hittites, possibly even related, as the Hittites were Indo-European and used horses and speedy war chariots. Geography makes both theories unlikely. The Hittite homeland of Hatti was a thousand miles from Babylonia and even further from Iran's Zagros Mountains. What's more, the Kassites did not immediately take possession of Babylon after the Hittites left; they waited twenty-five years, which strains the credibility of a link between the two cultures.

This Kassite cylinder seal impression features a male worshiper, a dog, and a prayer in cuneiform script.

Metropolitan Museum of Art, CC0, via Wikimedia Commons;
https://commons.wikimedia.org/wiki/File:Cylinder_seal_and_modern_impression-
_male_worshiper,_dog_surmounted_by_a_standard_MET_ss1985_357_44.jpg

Wherever they were from, the Kassites took possession of Babylon and held it for four hundred years! Intriguingly, their first king, Agum Kakrîme (Agum II), marched one thousand miles northwest to the Hittite kingdom, crushed the Hittites, and stole back Marduk's statue. He returned Marduk to Babylon, rebuilt the Esagila (Esangil) temple, purified it by a snake charmer, built protective demons to guard the door, and installed Marduk's image in its rightful place. A scribe documented all of this in what is known as the *Agum Kakrîme Inscription.*

Some scholars question the authenticity of the *Agum Kakrîme Inscription.* Its two existing copies, unearthed in Nineveh, were written after the Kassite era but based on an original inscription. The copies were written in Akkadian (the written language of the

Babylonian Amorites and the Kassites) with the Neo-Assyrian cuneiform script (used after 900 BCE) but following a more ancient style. The main point of the inscription is Agum's legitimacy to rule Babylon and how he was the tender, attentive shepherd of all Babylon's people, regardless of ethnicity. He also asserts his dominance over the Alman, Gutians, and Padan: all tribes from the Zagros Mountains, which helps support that region as the Kassite home territory.

If the inscription is authentic, it says much about Agum's character and the Kassites. Traveling a two-thousand-mile round trip to retrieve the god of the previous civilization and return it to its restored temple reflects the profound respect of the Kassites for the vanquished Amorite-Babylonians. It also puts to rest the speculation that the Hittites and Kassites were in league.

Rescuing Marduk may have been a way for Agum to assert his legitimacy. Babylon was a holy city, and the Amorites had championed Marduk as the new head god of Mesopotamia's pantheon. Agum showed respect for the sacred temples and images. Marduk had replaced Enlil as the "king-making" god, so bringing Marduk "home" would win favor with Marduk and his followers. In addition to rebuilding Babylon, Agum also rebuilt Nippur, the most sacred city of the Sumerians from ancient times, and replicated all Nippur's temples that had fallen into ruin. Agum and the rest of the Kassite kings worshiped the Amorite god Marduk, the Sumerian gods such as Enlil, and their own chief deities, Šuqamuna and his wife, Šumaliya.

The "Dark Age" of Mesopotamia took place in the interim period after Babylon fell to the Hittites. This age marked political and cultural regress, with drastic changes to society and the Mesopotamian way of life. Before about 1400 BCE, we have sparse documentation of what happened in the earliest days of Kassite rule in Babylon, including no documentation in the Kassite language and almost nothing in any other language.

Were the Kassites literate when they took possession of Babylon? Since no inscriptions or cuneiform tablets have been found in the Kassite language, they presumably had no written language of their own. They adopted the Babylonian-Akkadian dialect for legal documents and used the virtually extinct Sumerian language for some monuments. This may have been a way to honor the preceding civilizations, as the Kassites seemed determined to do, perhaps as a way to preserve their legitimacy. Some Kassites lived in Babylonia and Sumer before rising to power; they may have already used the Babylonian and Sumerian written languages.

The lack of documentation for this age may stem from a loss of literacy in the ruling classes. It may also relate to the destruction of documents, either by rival kings' invasions or environmental conditions. Babylon's underground water table is quite near the surface. While the cuneiform tablets and other artifacts of Mesopotamia fared well in other places with desert conditions, they disintegrated in the lower levels of Babylon's ruins, aided by several significant floods of Babylon through the millennia. Even if they still survive in the watery depths under Babylon, getting to them is a challenge.

The data we have for the earliest Kassite era in Babylon come from several contemporary sources, including the *Assyrian King List*, which has a few notations of interactions with Kassite-ruled Babylonia. Another contemporary Assyrian document is the *Synchronistic History (ABC)*, which records two treaties between the Assyrian and Kassite kings. The *Chronicles of the Early Kings* was written later, in the Neo-Babylonian age, but provides information on the Kassite kings. However, the further back in time one goes in this document, the more dubious the information becomes.

Only three important artifacts have been unearthed from the Dark Age of the early Kassite period in Babylon. These were a mace head and a stone frog, both with inscriptions to Ula-burarias, son of King Burna-burarias of Sealand. The mace head was found in a more recent Parthian-period house in Babylon, and the frog was found in the Ararat plain of Armenia.[21] Although King Burna-burarias is called the king of Sealand in both inscriptions, he was also the second king of Babylon. Twenty tablets excavated from the island of Bahrain in the Persian Gulf named King Agum the first Kassite king of Babylonia. He succeeded where the Amorites had failed by conquering the Sealand Dynasty and also gaining control of Bahrain, which had been under Sealand's domination.

The early Kassite kings of Babylonia conquered Sumer within their first sixty-five years of rule. Sumer was no longer a network of combative city-states but one large, unified province. The Kassites then began pressing north into what is present-day Baghdad. Expanding north brought them into conflict with the Assyrians, so Agum's successor Burna-burarias I negotiated a treaty with Assyria regarding the border between Babylonia and Assyria.

---

[21] Frans van Koppen, "The Old to Middle Babylonian Transition: History and Chronology of the Mesopotamian Dark Age." *Ägypten Und Levante / Egypt and the Levant* 20 (2010): 455. http://www.jstor.org/stable/23789952

The Ziggurat of Dur-Kurigalzu once stood in the Kassite capital.
https://commons.wikimedia.org/wiki/File:%E2%80%98Aqar_Q%C5%ABf.jpg

As the Kassite kingdom of Babylonia grew in territory and control of profitable trade routes, its exponential wealth led King Kurigalzu I to construct a splendid new 560-acre royal city, Dur-Kurigalzu, with gleaming palaces and temples. The ruins of the Ziggurat of Dur-Kurigalzu still tower over the desert close to Baghdad. Babylonia now stretched almost a thousand miles from Bahrain (Dilmun) in the south to the border of Assyria in the north. Babylon was also enjoying unprecedented and lengthy stability and peace, with rewarding trade with neighbors such as the Assyrians and Mitanni of northern Mesopotamia and Elam to the east.

Kurigalzu and his descendants also corresponded regularly and traded with more distant kingdoms like Egypt, Anatolia, the Hittite Empire, Greece, and Armenia. The *Amarna Letters*, a collection of cuneiform tablets found in Egypt, include correspondence between the Egyptian pharaohs and the Kassite kings, fourteen letters where they affectionately called each other "brother," exchanged gifts, and arranged royal marriages. The Kassite royalty intermarried with the royal families of Egypt, Elam, Assyria, and Hatti (western Turkey). These other powerful kingdoms recognized Babylon as an equal.

The Kassites were master assimilators, so much so that they left little of their own cultural trace behind. They thoughtfully followed the Mesopotamian customs and practices, yet they did leave their unique stamp in the arts. One innovation was glazing bricks, which became a hallmark of Babylonian artwork on their city walls, gates, palaces, and temples through the Neo-Babylonian and Achaemenid periods.

Babylonia's wide-reaching trade and friendship with far-flung lands brought in lapis lazuli and other brilliantly-colored semiprecious stones. The Kassites used these beautiful stones in their artwork with cylinder seals, which featured tall, thin figures, exquisitely engraved prayers, and gold caps at the end of the cylinders. The Kassites also devoted careful attention to restoring ancient temples, following the exact model of what had once stood there. Curiously, they often used the Sumerian language for inscriptions on cornerstones and victory steles, even though the language had barely been used for centuries. They considered themselves stewards of the past Sumerian, Akkadian, and Babylonian civilizations, meticulously preserving ancient documents, literature, and religious artifacts.

One type of monument the Kassites innovated was *kudurrus*: polished stones gracing the inside of temples with inscriptions of pivotal real estate transactions. They decorated the kudurrus stones with Mesopotamian and Kassite deities. The kudurrus were a Kassite legacy that endured long after their reign in Babylon ended.

On this Kassite kudurra, King Meli-Shipak II presents his daughter to the deity Ḫunnubat-Nanaya.

https://commons.wikimedia.org/wiki/File:Kudurru_Melishipak_Louvre_Sb23_n02.jpg

Murder and mayhem struck the Kassite palace in 1333 BCE. Shortly after Kara-hardas ascended Babylon's throne, a military coup d'état overthrew his government. The rebels killed the young king and installed the usurper Nazi-Bugash on the throne. The murder infuriated the Assyrian king Assur-uballit. His daughter Muballitat-Serua was married to the previous Kassite king, and the renegades had killed his grandson, Kara-hardas.

A vengeful Assur-uballit marched his Assyrian army south, invaded Babylonia, executed the usurper, and installed Kurigalzu II, another grandson and the slain Kara-hardas' brother, as Babylonia's new king. The boy-king was essentially a vassal to his grandfather. Despite the blood ties between Assyria and Babylonia, acrimony grew as the young king matured. After his grandfather died and his uncle Enlil-nīrāri ascended the throne, Kurigalzu II went to war against Assyria and lost the battle. He also lost territory as the boundary lines between the two kingdoms were adjusted in Assyria's favor.

After several more years of intermittent battles between the Assyrians and Kassites, they declared a truce so Assyria could deal with the Mitanni and Hittites. King Shalmaneser I successfully defeated the coalition Mitanni and Hittite forces and gouged out one eye from each of his 14,400 war prisoners. While Assyria was at war with other enemies, the Kassites enjoyed peace, with Nippur especially flourishing.

The Kassites' brief peace came crashing to an end when Tukulti-Ninurta I ascended Assyria's throne. After trouncing the Hittites, he marched south to deal with the Babylonians, who had been disrespecting the boundary lines with Assyria while he'd been busy with the Hittites. He flattened Babylon's walls, massacred the Kassites, and stole Marduk's statue. He hauled the naked and chained Kassite king and his harem back to Assyria as prisoners and ruled over Babylonia himself for eight years, from 1235 to 1227 BCE. Two decades later, Tukulti-Ninurta's own sons staged a coup and stabbed him to death. In the chaos, the Babylonians somehow managed to get Marduk back, perhaps voluntarily returned by the Assyrians!

Around 1200 BCE, the Bronze Age Collapse struck the Middle East, North Africa, Greece, and Turkey. A series of environmental events, including drought, earthquakes, tsunamis, and volcanic eruptions, disrupted civilizations, leading to population shifts and the sudden decline of once-great political powers. The "Sea People" of unknown origin besieged the Mediterranean coastal areas, violently destroying cities in Canaan, Lebanon, Syria, and Turkey. During this era, the stately cities of Mycenean Greece lay abandoned, and the Hittite Empire crumbled. In Mesopotamia, Assyria survived—even thrived—but the Kassite Dynasty declined.

Meanwhile, the Elamites began stirring up trouble. The Elamite and Kassite royal families had been intermarrying for generations, and the Elamites claimed their blood ties to Babylonia as justification for invading and claiming their "rightful throne" in 1150

BCE. They captured Enlil-nadin-ahi, Babylonia's last Kassite king, and took him as a prisoner to Susa. They also stole Marduk's idol and carried him away: the third time Marduk was stolen!

After the Elamites successfully took Babylon, the fleeing Kassites rallied at Isin. With Isin's assistance, they launched a counterattack, drove the Elamites out of Babylonia, and ruled in Dynasty IV of Babylon (1153–1022 BCE). By this time, all of Mesopotamia was feeling the effects of the prolonged drought and other factors of the Bronze Age Collapse. Most cities emptied, except Babylon, Ur, and Isin.

A century of chaos followed when the Arameans invaded, ending Kassite rule in Babylonia forever. Most of the Kassites retreated to the Lorestan region of the Zagros Mountains in Iran, where centuries later, the Assyrian King Sennacherib fought them in 702 BCE. However, some Kassites remained in Babylonia and held important positions in later dynasties. During their own reign, the Kassites had honored the previous Amorite, Sumerian, and Akkadian civilizations, and the later rulers of Babylon likewise esteemed the Kassites.

Chapter 5: The Assyrian Rule

Babylonia existed south of its neighbor Assyria, usually in an uneasy truce. The royal families intermarried and allied against common enemies, yet peace was tenuous. Babylon and Assyria exercised dominance over one other in a constantly shifting power play in which the fierce Assyrians usually had the upper hand.

The Assyrians struck fear into their neighbors for two millennia, even terrorizing nations a thousand miles away. They created the largest empire in the world at that time and, like Babylon, passed through several eras of extensive sovereignty in the Middle East, followed by horrendous falls. Who were the Assyrians? The *Torah* said the Semitic shepherds living by the Tigris River were the descendants of Ashur, the son of Shem and grandson of Noah.[22] They spoke an Akkadian dialect, and their original city was Assur (Ashur).

Sargon the Great conquered the fledgling town of Assur and probably founded Babylon around the same time. After the Akkadian Empire fell, Assur (although not the northern Assyrian settlements like Nineveh) and Babylon came under the Third

---

[22] *Genesis 10:22,* Tanakh: Torah: Bereishit.

Dynasty of Ur's dominance. Then, under King Puzur-Ashur I, around 2025 BCE, Assyria grew into a modest, independent city-state with approximately ten thousand people. Babylon gained independence about two centuries later under the Amorite king Sumu-Abum.

In 1808 BCE, an Amorite usurper, Shamshi-Adad, grabbed power in Assyria and expanded the unassuming group of city-states into an empire that stretched northwest into Turkey and Syria. But toward the end of Shamshi-Adad's reign, Hammurabi ascended the Babylonian throne and rapidly transformed Babylon into a dominant kingdom over Assyria and Sumer. Under Hammurabi's long reign, Assyria's subsequent three kings were vassals to Babylon.

Assyria regained independence after Hammurabi died, although it entered chaotic self-rule with multiple usurpers for several years until the Adaside Dynasty gained power in Assyria and held it for almost one thousand years. The Hittites bypassed Assyria to invade and plunder Babylon, after which it fell under Kassite rule. Meanwhile, Assyria endured a couple of decades of dominance by the Mitanni.

When the Assyrians shook off the Mitanni, they made a treaty with the Kassite Babylonians, rebuilt Assur, and reestablished their advanced trade system. Shortly after, in 1392 BCE, King Eriba-Adad I ascended the Assyrian throne, which marked the beginning of the Middle Assyrian Empire (1392–1056). At this point, Babylon was in its Kassite era (Middle Babylon). Assyria rebounded phenomenally, seizing most of the western Turkey homeland of its bitter rivals, the Hittites, and northern Mesopotamia, Syria, Lebanon, and Canaan.

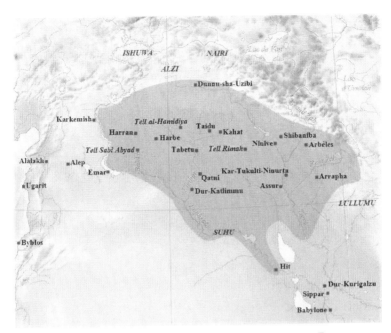

This map shows the location of the Middle Assyrian Dynasty.
Near_East_topographic_map-blank.svg: Sémhurderivative work: Zunkir, CC BY-SA 3.0 https://creativecommons.org/licenses/by-sa/3.0 via Wikimedia Commons; https://commons.wikimedia.org/wiki/File:M%C3%A9dio-assyrien.png

In a desperate attempt to regain control, the Hittites unsuccessfully allied with Babylon against Assyria. In the 1245 BCE Battle of Nihriya, Tukulti-Ninurta decimated the Hittites, capturing and enslaving 28,800 prisoners. He then wreaked his revenge on Babylon by flattening its walls, massacring the population, and plundering its temples in what both the Babylonians and Assyrians considered a frightful act of sacrilege. However, Tukulti-Ninurta justified his actions in the *Tukulti-Ninurta Epic*, claiming the Babylonians offended the gods by breaking oaths and disregarding their treaty with Assyria.

The Assyrians, however, were aghast at Tukulti-Ninurta's desecration of the sacred city, and especially of his stealing Marduk from Babylon. They trembled in fear of what Marduk might do to them. When Tukulti-Ninurta's sons murdered him, the Assyrians nodded to themselves: he'd brought disaster down by his impiety.

Tukulti-Ninurta's death prompted Babylonia, which had been a tribute-paying vassal kingdom, to declare independence.

Mesopotamia had entered into the Bronze Age Collapse by this point, but it wasn't as devastated by environmental catastrophes and invasions by displaced people as the Mediterranean region. Nevertheless, the Kassites fell to the Elamites in the twelfth century. Babylon fell under Assyria's domination, with new populations of Arameans and Suteans moving into Babylonia, fleeing the drought and Sea People invasions along the Mediterranean. Assyria began weakening with internecine conflict, holding tenuous control over Babylon.

In 1121 BCE, King Nebuchadnezzar I of Isin took possession of Babylon and ruled for twenty-two years (not to be confused with the more-famous Nebuchadnezzar II of the Neo-Babylonian era and biblical fame). King Nebuchadnezzar made a failed attempt at invading Elam, interrupted when the plague hit and routed his troops. His second try was an insane surprise attack in the heat of the desert summer, tramping over scorching roads with dried-up water holes and their metal weapons burning like fire in their hands. His madness paid off: the Elamites were unprepared and never recovered from the attack. The best part of the raid was that he recovered Marduk, whom the Elamites had stolen from Babylon three decades earlier.

This kudurru stone tells of Nebuchadnezzar's rescue of Marduk from the Elamites.

Flushed with victory over the Elamites, Nebuchadnezzar I set his sights on Assyria. He had initially existed harmoniously with Assyria's King Ashur-resh-ishi I (1133–1116 BCE). However, Nebuchadnezzar I later broke his treaty and besieged two Assyrian cities, a dismal failure. He was no match for the forceful and brilliant military tactics of Ashur-resh-ishi, who chased him out of Assyria.

Ashur-resh-ishi's son Tiglath-Pileser I was even more invincible than his father. He transformed Assyria's military into the Middle East's preeminent power in his forty-one-year reign. After overcoming the Arameans in Syria, he charged through Phoenicia's maritime cities, conquering Byblos, Berytus (Beirut), Tyre, and Sidon along the Mediterranean. After rebuilding and restoring Assyria's neglected temples, he dedicated them through the human sacrifice of "precious victims."

While Tiglath-Pileser was off fighting in foreign lands, Nebuchadnezzar I daringly attempted raids in Assyria. When Tiglath-Pileser heard of Nebuchadnezzar's audacity, he charged back to Mesopotamia, lay siege to Babylonia's cities, and destroyed Nebuchadnezzar's palace in Babylon—but left the city's temples untouched. He would not repeat Tukulti-Ninurta's mistake of incurring the gods' wrath.

Tiglath-Pileser's son Ashur-bel-Kala received a friendly visit from Babylon's King Marduk-šāpik-zēri at his coronation, and they allied against their common enemy: the Arameans. Five years later, Marduk-šāpik-zēri died, and Ashur-bel-Kala put a puppet king on Babylon's throne. The last king of the Middle Assyrian Empire, Ashur-bel-Kala, was forced to defend his realm against a usurper: Tukulti-Mer. He finally gave the pretender the boot, but the Hittites and Arameans took Phoenicia and Syria while he was distracted by internal affairs. This loss began a one-century Assyrian slump, during which it lost Babylonia and all territory except the original Assyrian cities.

The Assyrians' skilled horsemanship led to victory in war and the hunt.
Carole Raddato from FRANKFURT, Germany, CC BY-SA 2.0
https://creativecommons.org/licenses/by-sa/2.0 via Wikimedia Commons;
https://commons.wikimedia.org/wiki/File:Exhibition_I_am_Ashurbanipal_king_of_t
he_world,_king_of_Assyria,_British_Museum_(31033563287).jpg

Assyria recovered from its nosedive when Adad-nirari II (911–891 BCE) ascended the throne as the first king of the Neo-Assyrian period. For three centuries, the Neo-Assyrian Empire exponentially expanded, overpowering all of Mesopotamia and the eastern Mediterranean coastline from Turkey to Egypt. One component of their success was their advanced siege engines that struck terror into the hearts of rival cities huddled behind their city walls.

The Assyrians' revolutionary use of iron weapons and war chariots also contributed to a nearly indomitable army. The Mesopotamians, Egyptians, and Hittites had been using iron found in meteorites for two millennia, but around 1300 BCE, the cultures of the Near East began developing iron smelting and smithing technology. Iron weapons and chariots were of a higher caliber than bronze, which had to be cast, making it more brittle. The stronger iron weapons were made from hammering heated iron ore, which was readily available. Bronze was cast from copper and tin; although copper was available in Mesopotamia (but not as common as iron ore), tin deposits were rare and usually imported.

Because iron ore was five hundred times more common than copper in Mesopotamia, once the Assyrians developed iron smelting, cold forging, and tempering technologies, they could afford to outfit entire massive armies with iron weapons. Coupled with formidable siege engines, logistical capabilities, and strategic tactics, the Assyrian iron chariots and weapons made it the most advanced military of the day.

Beginning with the astute leadership of King Adad-Nirari II, Assyria's incredible conquering force took one nation after another. City by city, the Assyrians used wheeled siege towers, battering rams, mobile ladders, and earthen ramps to breach city walls. They even dug tunnels under the walls! Adad-Nirari led two campaigns into Babylonia, capturing extensive territory north of the Diyala River and forming a treaty with Babylon that ensured peace for several generations. However, his successors destroyed and reconquered Babylon multiple times.

Adad-Nirari's grandson, the diabolically cruel Ashurnasirpal II, aggressively extended the empire, beginning in the Armenian highlands. From there, he marched on Syria, overcame the Neo-Hittites and Aramaeans, and then entered into diplomatic relations with Phoenicia and Israel. He continued the diplomatic ties with Babylon that his grandfather established, for which they were no doubt grateful, considering his treatment of other regions.

Ashurnasirpal II's palace stood in Nimrud for three millennia before ISIL bulldozed it in 2015;
https://commons.wikimedia.org/wiki/File:Iraq;_Nimrud_-_Assyria,_Lamassu%27s_Guarding_Palace_Entrance.jpg

Whenever a city revolted against Ashurnasirpal's harsh rule and heavy tribute requirements, they would receive his horrific retribution, beginning the shock and terror methods that Assyrians would use for the next few centuries. When the city of Tela in Syria resisted him, Ashurnasirpal cruelly crushed the citizens with actions he would repeatedly use to squash rebellion:

"I built a pillar over against the city gate, and I flayed all the chiefs who had revolted, and I covered the pillar with their skins. Some I impaled upon the pillar on stakes, and others I bound to stakes around the pillar. I cut the limbs off the officers who had rebelled. Many captives I burned with fire, and many I took as living captives. From some, I cut off their noses, their ears, and their fingers; of many, I put out their eyes. I made one pillar of the living and another of heads, and I bound their heads to tree trunks round about the city. Their young men and maidens I consumed with fire. The rest of their warriors I consumed with thirst in the desert of the Euphrates."[23]

Ashurnasirpal's son, Shalmaneser III, led a 70,000-man force with 4,000 chariots and 1,200 horsemen. Large cavalry forces were a novelty and probably used mercenaries from Turkey and the Zagros Mountains. The Assyrian military grew to 200,000 soldiers in the next few generations, the largest army in the Middle East up to that point. Although most of their military were farmers called up for duty, the Assyrians began training specialized forces, engineers, and spies.

Shalmaneser III continued the peace treaty with Babylon that Adad-Nirari had established. However, Babylonia experienced a coup d'état when King Marduk-zakir-shumi's younger brother Marduk-bel-usate tried to usurp the throne. Shalmaneser marched to Babylonia to defend his ally, and the rebel brother fled to the mountains, where Shalmaneser pursued him and cut him down with his sword.

Shalmaneser also encountered a palace coup when his son Assur-danin-pal attempted to steal his throne, grasping power over twenty-seven Assyrian cities and allying with the Babylonian king Marduk-balassu-iqbi. Another son of Shalmaneser, Shamshi-Adad V, defended Shalmaneser (who died after two years) and continued with a four-year power struggle against his brother, which he finally won, although with a much-weakened Assyria.

Shamshi-Adad then led two revenge campaigns against Babylon. In his first campaign, after taking time out for a lion hunt (a favorite Assyrian pastime), he wreaked havoc on northern Babylonia until the coalition forces of Babylonians, Chaldeans, Elamites, Arameans, and Kassites fought him off. In his second campaign

---

[23] Joshua J. Mark, "Ashurnasirpal II," *World History Encyclopedia.*
https://www.worldhistory.org/Ashurnasirpal_II/

against Babylon, Shamshi-Adad captured King Marduk-balāssu-iqbi and dragged him to Assyria in chains.

Tiglath-Pileser III became the joint king of Assyria and Babylon.
Osama Shukir Muhammed Amin FRCP(Glasg), CC BY-SA 4.0
https://creativecommons.org/licenses/by-sa/4.0 via Wikimedia Commons;
https://commons.wikimedia.org/wiki/File:Tiglath-pileser_III,_an_alabaster_bas-
relief_from_the_king%27s_central_palace_at_Nimrud,_Mesopotamia.JPG

For sixty-five years, Assyria struggled to recover from the impact of its civil war. In 745 BCE, Tiglath-Pileser III received the Assyrian crown and immediately set to work restoring Assyria to power, recovering the breakaway provinces, including Israel, and engaging in population-relocation programs to ward off any further rebellion:

> "King Pul of Assyria (also known as Tiglath-Pileser) invaded the land and took the people of Reuben, Gad, and the half-tribe of Manasseh as captives. The Assyrians exiled them to Halah, Habor, Hara, and the Gozan River, where they remain to this day."[24]

[24] *1 Chronicles 5:26,* Tanakh: Book of Divrei HaYamim I.

"In the days of Pekah, king of Israel, came Tiglath-Pileser king of Assyria and took Ijon, Abel-beth-maacah, Janoah, and Kedesh, and Hazor, and Gilead, and Galilee, all the land of Naphtali; and he carried them captive to Assyria."[25]

Tiglath-Pileser then turned his attention to Babylonia. Like Assyria, Babylonia had been experiencing a period of stagnation, lacking the military power that Assyria had built up. It engaged in ongoing power struggles with the Chaldeans who had migrated into Mesopotamia from the Levant (Syria, Lebanon, Israel) beginning in the tenth century BCE and were settling in southeastern Babylonia. The Chaldeans spoke a western Semitic language, similar to Aramaean.

In the 8th century BCE, three Chaldean tribal leaders, apparently unrelated, gained ascendency over Babylonia, ruling as kings during the power vacuum created by conflict with Assyria. One of these Chaldean kings, Erība-Marduk, helped restore order to Babylonia after a prolonged period of instability. He reverenced Babylon's god Marduk by restoring his throne in the Esagila temple.

Two years after Tiglath-Pileser III ascended Assyria's throne, Nabonassar deposed a Chaldean ruler and became king of Babylonia. Two years later, in 745 BCE, Tiglath-Pileser invaded Babylonia, pillaging the cities of Hamranu and Rabbilu and stealing their gods. He destroyed the major Chaldean city of Bit-Shilani, skewered its ruler, and subdued the Aramaeans and Chaldeans. Tiglath-Pileser did not bother Nabonassar; in fact, the Babylonian king may have invited Tiglath-Pileser's assistance—he certainly benefited from the Assyrian king trouncing his rivals.

The next few years in Babylonia's history featured insurrection, dynastic overthrow, and usurpation. Another Chaldean, Nabu-mukin-zeri, crowned himself king in 731 BCE, much to Tiglath-Pileser's annoyance. Nabu-mukin-zeri immediately set about

---

[25] *2 Kings 15:29,* Tanakh: Book of Malachim II.

mediating the differences between the various Babylonian ethnic and political groups. Tiglath-Pileser preferred Babylonia to be disconnected and at odds so it could not rival Assyria.

Tiglath-Pileser set out to overthrow Nabu-mukin-zeri, first installing a blockade to the east to prevent Elam from getting involved. He then conquered several Aramean and Chaldean tribes. In 730 BCE, he sent his envoys to urge the city of Babylon to surrender, promising tax privileges, but to no avail. In 729 BCE, Tiglath-Pileser lay siege and took Babylon, declaring himself king of both Assyria and Babylonia, although Nabu-mukin-zeri continued to resist for several years. Tiglath-Pileser kept all of Babylonia, which comprised most of central and southern Mesopotamia, as one united vassal kingdom to Assyria. He honored the Babylonian deities, temples, and culture, attending religious festivals in Babylon.

Tiglath-Pileser's son Shalmaneser V spent most of his short, five-year reign (727–722 BCE) campaigning in Israel. He dealt with unruly kingdoms by implementing the population-relocation programs used by his father. He evacuated the Samarian province of northern Israel and resettled them in Assyria and Babylonia. He then exiled some of the troublesome tribal groups in Assyria and Babylonia to Samaria.[26] This created a wholly different Mesopotamian ethnicity and religion in Samaria, at odds with the rest of Israel even in Jesus's day centuries later. It also meant that a large Jewish population lived in Babylon (from this and other population-relocation endeavors), and some rose to positions of power and influence with the Babylonian kings.

Sargon II ruled Assyria next, probably usurping the throne from his brother. Despite Shalmaneser's population relocations, the Babylonian king Marduk-apla-iddina proved insubordinate to Assyrian rule, forcing Sargon II to reconquer the kingdom. Before a military invasion, Sargon astutely used secret negotiations with the

---

[26] *2 Kings 17:24-41*, Tanakh: Malachim II.

northern Babylonian tribes and cities to forge alliances. He then marched along the Tigris River to southern Babylonia to conquer Dur-Abi-hara. He successfully negotiated again to win over the southern Babylonians from that stronghold.

Marduk-apla-iddina fled to Elam, and the cheering people of Babylon opened their city gates to Sargon II. Fortunately for the Babylonians, Sargon was not as savage as his predecessors: he did not punish the rebels as harshly and even extended the rights of Assyrian citizenship in a relationship in which Assyria was considered the husband and Babylonia the wife. He lived in Babylon for the next three years, engaging in the traditional religious ceremonies and improving the infrastructure.

Sargon II died in battle in Anatolia, and his body disappeared; in the chaos, his men could not recover it. Many perceived the lack of proper funeral rites as a bad omen, and rebellions sprung up around the Assyrian Empire, which Sargon's son Sennacherib struggled to subdue. Babylonia refused to be a submissive "wife": the people felt he'd disrespected Marduk by refusing to "take the hand" of the god.

Sennacherib subdued the rebellion and installed a vassal king, Bel-ibni: a Babylonian who had grown up in his palace. That didn't go well; the young king almost immediately began conspiring with the Chaldeans and Elamites, so Sennacherib exiled him to Assyria. He put his son, Ashur-nadin-shumi, on Babylonia's throne, but that didn't go well either. The Elamites invaded, killed the young king, and, once again, stole Marduk.

Another son of Sennacherib, Esarhaddon, became king of Assyria and Babylon. He retrieved Marduk from the Elamites and rebuilt the Esagila temple and the city of Babylon, living in Babylon part of the time. After Esarhaddon died, his oldest son Shamash-shum-ukin ruled Babylon while a younger son Ashurbanipal ruled Assyria from Nineveh. The brothers fell into a civil war, with the Elamites, Persians, Chaldeans, Canaanites, and Arabs supporting

Shamash-shum-ukin. Despite the massive coalition forces, Ashurbanipal won the war.

Ashurbanipal laid siege to Babylon, and when the starving and disease-ridden population surrendered, he killed his brother by burning him to death, then appointed an Assyrian as governor of Babylonia. He dismembered his brother's concubines and officials and fed their body parts to the vultures and dogs. Ashurbanipal also took many of Babylon's ancient texts to Nineveh, where he installed them in his massive library, preserving them for history. He was the last of Assyria's great kings; the empire crumbled shortly after his death.

While Assyria was deteriorating, Babylonia was rising in power once again. Of uncertain origins, calling himself the "son of nobody," Nabopolassar took advantage of Assyria's weakness to stage a revolt. Nabopolassar's first strikes were against Nippur and Babylon, which he swiftly conquered. The Assyrians wasted no time in counterattacking, taking Nippur back. However, they found Nabopolassar too strong when they attacked Babylon and Uruk. He crowned himself king in 626 BCE, freeing Babylonia from centuries of vassalage under Assyrian rule.

Chapter 6: A New Empire – The Neo-Babylonians

A phenomenal power shift rocked Assyria when Nabopolassar seized power over Babylon in 626 BCE. This marked the beginning of the short-lived but dynamic Neo-Babylonian Empire, known for its scientific and mathematic breakthroughs, brilliant architecture, and interactions with Judah, Tyre, and Egypt, as recorded in the Hebrew Tanakh (Old Testament). While the sensational Neo-Babylonian exploded unto the Middle Eastern scene, the Neo-Assyrian Empire drifted into its twilight years, to eventually be snuffed out altogether.

The Assyrian king Sinsharishkun desperately attempted to regain dominance over Babylonia in 625-623 BCE. His counteroffensives in northern Babylonia were initially successful: he conquered Sippar and held Nippur from Nabopolassar's assaults. However, trouble loomed to the east. Elam had been a vassal to Assyria but now threw off its shackles, cut off tribute payments, and joined forces with Nabopolassar. Sinsharishkun responded by amassing a gigantic army to meet the new threat and spectacularly retook Uruk.

Just when Sinsharishkun thought that triumph over Babylon was in his hand, he received disturbing news. One of his own generals from the western provinces had revolted and was marching on Assyria's capital city of Nineveh. With most of Assyria's military in the far south, Nineveh's small army did not even try to defend the city. The unnamed usurper crowned himself Assyria's new king, forcing Sinsharishkun to abandon his campaign in Babylonia and rush home to confront his challenger.

After several months of brutal civil war, Sinsharishkun ejected the interloper, but the Babylonians took advantage of his absence to lay siege to Uruk and Nippur. Desperate for food, the Assyrians finally surrendered the cities, but not before some citizens made the agonizing choice between selling their children into slavery or watching them starve. Nabopolassar then wreaked havoc on the remaining Assyrian garrisons in the south; they all capitulated by 620 BCE. After chasing out the Assyrians, Nabopolassar now securely held all Babylonia.

While the Assyrians and Babylonians had been experiencing coup d'états and viciously struggling for control of Babylonia, new powers were rising to the east. The Medes, a tribe in today's northwestern Iran, were taking advantage of Elam's weakness to expand their territory. As the Assyrian Empire unraveled, the Medes stopped the tribute they'd paid Assyria for centuries.

To avenge his father's death by the Assyrians, King Cyaxares of Media staged a frontal assault on Assyria's capital of Nineveh. In the midst of their barrage on Nineveh, the Scythians launched a surprise attack on the Medes' rear, led by King Madyas. Who were the Scythians? They were fierce nomadic shepherds from the Eurasian steppes north of the Black Sea in today's Kazakhstan, Russia, and Ukraine. These bloodthirsty, expert horsemen were staging savage raids on northern Mesopotamia but had allied with Assyria.

This Greek vase features a Scythian archer painted by Epiktetos,
520-500 BCE.
https://commons.wikimedia.org/wiki/File:Skythian_archer_plate_BM_E135_by_Epiktetos.jpg

The Scythians pummeled the Medes, forcing them to bow to their overlordship. For a few years, the Medes had no choice but to pay tribute to the Scythians and leave Assyria unmolested. But in 625 BCE, Cyaxares schemed to break the Scythian yoke. He invited the Scythian nobility to a grand feast, serving them full-strength wine while the Medes drank watered-down wine. When the Scythian lords were roaring drunk, the Medes attacked and killed them all. With their leadership wiped out, the Scythians pragmatically joined forces with the Medes. Together, they launched another siege on Nineveh and took the city.

Nine years later, having consolidated all of Babylonia, Nabopolassar dared to invade Assyrian territory in 616 BCE. Following the Euphrates north into Syria, he took Assyrian cities up to the Khabur River. The Assyrians called on their ally, Egypt's Pharoah Psamtik I, who preferred having the Assyrians controlling the Levant, providing safer borders for Egypt with its northern neighbors. Psamtik marched north to merge his mammoth military with Assyria's.

Babylonia had not been much of a threat to other empires for centuries, so it came as a shock when the coalition Assyrian-Egyptian forces lost the first battle to the Babylonian upstarts. Disconcerted, the Egyptians backed off, forcing Assyria to withdraw and leaving Babylonia in control of the middle Euphrates. This gave Babylonia unlimited access to the prosperous trade routes and provided a buffer zone against an Assyrian attack on Babylonia. With that accomplished, Nabopolassar halted any further invasion of Assyria for the time being.

Before plotting his next step against Assyria, Nabopolassar needed to negotiate strategic alliances. He already had Chaldean support, and in 616 BCE, he allied with Cyaxares, king of the Medes and great-grandfather of Cyrus the Great. As part of the treaty, Nabopolassar's son, Nebuchadnezzar II, married Cyaxares' daughter, Princess Amytis, and Cyaxares married Nabopolassar's daughter. The Medes brought the Scythians with them to the Babylonian side.

Nabopolassar then marched into Assyria's heartland, attacking Assur, the Assyrian's first city, one-time capital, and sacred home of their principal god Ashur. Sinsharishkun hurriedly mustered his forces, marched to Assur, and forced Nabopolassar into retreat. But then King Cyaxares led the Medes into Assyria in 614 BCE and launched a horrific attack on Assur. He brutally conquered the city, massacring the citizens and pillaging the sacred temples. Nabopolassar arrived after the city was taken, appalled by Cyaxares' ruthlessness and disregard for the holy sites.

As dreadful as the sacking of Assur was for the Assyrians, the horror had only begun. In 612 BCE, a staggering coalition force of Babylonians, Chaldeans, Cimmerians, Medes, Persians, Sagartians, and Scythians launched a full-scale invasion of Assyria. The Cimmerians were from southwest Asia and had assimilated with the

Scythians, while the Sagartians were from the Iranian plateau. After laying siege to Nineveh for three months, the united forces ground its walls to dust, killed the Assyrian king Sinsharishkun, and destroyed the city, carrying off immense treasure from the palace and temples. Nahum, the prophet, described the desolation:

"Your enemy is coming to crush you, Nineveh. Man the ramparts! Watch the roads! Prepare your defenses! Call out your forces!

Shields flash red in the sunlight! See the scarlet uniforms of the valiant troops! Watch as their glittering chariots move into position, with a forest of spears waving above them. The chariots race recklessly along the streets and rush wildly through the squares. They flash like firelight and move as swiftly as lightning.

The king shouts to his officers; they stumble in their haste, rushing to the walls to set up their defenses. The river gates have been torn open! The palace is about to collapse! Nineveh's exile has been decreed, and all the servant girls mourn its capture. They moan like doves and beat their breasts in sorrow. Nineveh is like a leaking water reservoir! The people are slipping away. 'Stop, stop!' someone shouts, but no one even looks back.

Loot the silver! Plunder the gold! There's no end to Nineveh's treasures—its vast, uncounted wealth. Soon the city is plundered, empty, and ruined. Hearts melt, and knees shake. The people stand aghast, their faces pale and trembling."[27]

The Cimmerians, Medes, and Scythians stormed the rest of the Assyrian heartland, flattening the cities and defiling the temples. Nabopolassar and the Babylonians shared many of the same deities

---

[27] *Nahum 2,* Tanakh: Navi: Trei Assar.

with Assyria and found the sacrilege disturbing. The merciless attack on Assyria's homeland left only a minuscule remnant of a once-thriving population. The Cimmerians, Medes, and Scythians then charged into the Levant, laying waste to Turkey, Judah, and Israel, all the way south to Egypt's coastline.

The Babylonians utterly defeated the Assyrians and Egyptians in the Battle of Carchemish.
Credit: Patrick Gray, CC BY 2.0 https://creativecommons.org/licenses/by/2.0 via Wikimedia Commons; https://commons.wikimedia.org/wiki/File:Battle_of_Carchemish.png

The surviving Assyrian nobility escaped to Harran in Turkey, where they holed out, desperately seeking the aid of Egypt's Pharoah, Necho II. After consolidating their victory in Assyria, the Babylonian-Median forces marched on Harran in 610 BCE. As they approached, the Assyrians fled into Syria's desert. Necho II marched north from Egypt to rescue the Assyrian remnant, but Judah's King Josiah refused to let him pass through his country. Necho killed Josiah in the Battle of Megiddo, but the delay doomed the Assyrians.

The Babylonian coalition forces conquered Harran before Necho got there. When Necho arrived, the Babylonian crown prince Nebuchadnezzar led the Babylonian army in a lethal assault on Necho II and the few remaining Assyrians, wiping out the

Egyptian military to the last man. Assyria had fallen, and Egypt was brought to its knees, but the formidable Neo-Babylonian Empire rose as Mesopotamia's new shining star.

Shortly after the staggering victory against Egypt, Nabopolassar died, and Nebuchadnezzar II returned home as the war hero to ascend Babylon's throne in 605 BCE. He ruled for forty-three years as the Neo-Babylonian Empire's greatest king. Babylonia now held power over Assyria and all Mesopotamia, and Nebuchadnezzar would eventually subjugate western Saudi Arabia, Syria, Lebanon, Israel, Jordan, southern Turkey, and eastern Iran.

Nabopolassar's legacy to his son was stability in central and southern Mesopotamia, with the entire region under Babylonian control. Nebuchadnezzar swiftly consolidated the Assyrian heartland, subduing any remaining resistance and bringing all Mesopotamia under one throne. Nebuchadnezzar took advantage of this peace to expand and enhance his military and initiate stunning building projects around Babylonia, especially in the city of Babylon.

One nagging issue for Nebuchadnezzar II was the insubordinate kingdom of Judea. Over a century earlier, Shalmaneser V of Assyria had soundly defeated Judah's sister kingdom Israel, relocated most of its population to Assyria and Babylon, and resettled Israel with Mesopotamians. Judah remained independent until the Egyptian Pharoah Necho II killed King Josiah, making Judah a vassal to Egypt. But after Nebuchadnezzar destroyed Necho's army, he took control of Judah as a vassal kingdom while still crown prince.

Josiah's son Jehoiakim rebelled after three years of paying tribute, and Nebuchadnezzar, now Babylon's new king, marched to Judah to suppress the vassal king's rebellion. He defeated Jehoiakim and took some of the young men of Judah's royal family back to Babylon. These youths received Babylonian names, trained in the Babylonian language and literature for three years, then entered royal service. Four of these youths were Daniel

(Belteshazzar), Hananiah (Shadrach), Mishael (Meshach), and Azariah (Abednego). Daniel served as an advisor and dream interpreter to the Babylonian kings throughout the Neo-Babylonian Empire and briefly under Persian rule. Nebuchadnezzar appointed Daniel's three friends as leaders over the Babylonian provinces.[28]

After several years, the new king of Judah decided to throw off the yoke. In the eighth year of his reign, Nebuchadnezzar invaded Judah and took the young King Jehoiachin prisoner with his wives and the queen mother. He stripped the royal palace and the Jewish temple of the treasures of silver and gold accumulated centuries earlier by King Solomon. In what is known as the Babylonian Captivity, Nebuchadnezzar took ten thousand people of Jerusalem as captives back to Babylon—the military commanders, skilled soldiers, craftsmen, and artisans—leaving only the poorest people in the land. He installed Jehoiachin's uncle Zedekiah as a vassal king over Judah:[29]

> "By the rivers of Babylon, there we sat down, yea, we wept, when we remembered Zion. There on the willows, we hung our harps. For there our captors demanded of us songs, and our tormentors, jubilation, saying, 'Sing for us one of the songs of Zion!'"[30]

Despite the disastrous consequences his predecessors experienced when they rebelled, it wasn't long before Zedekiah, in league with Egypt and King Ithobaal III of Tyre, revolted. King Nebuchadnezzar laid siege to Jerusalem for two years as the people starved. Finally, King Zedekiah chanced a daring nighttime escape that ended in tragedy. The Babylonians captured him, forced him to watch his sons' executions, then gouged out his eyes and dragged him to Babylon in chains.[31]

---

[28] *Daniel 2*, Tanakh: Ketuvim: Book of Daniel.
[29] *2 Kings 24*, Tanakh: Navi: Book of Malachim II.
[30] *Psalm 137:1-3*, Tanakh: Ketuvim: Book of Tehillim.
[31] *2 Kings 25*.

Under Babylonian rule, the ancient city of Tyre on Lebanon's coast had enjoyed a few years of independence, except for paying tribute. The seaside Phoenician city had suffered under Assyrian rule, but under Nebuchadnezzar's more benevolent reign, it had been rebuilding its legendary wealth as a key trade center and harbor. Then Tyre's king joined forces with Egypt and Judah against Babylon: a foolhardy move. While laying siege to Judah, Nebuchadnezzar also besieged Tyre for thirteen long years, the last holdout in consolidating his empire. When Tyre finally surrendered, Nebuchadnezzar was amazingly merciful, allowing the city to continue as before with vassal kings. He astutely determined that the vast tribute he would receive from the city's affluent trade would enrich his empire.

Germany's Pergamon Museum displays this reproduction of the Ishtar Gate.
User: Hahaha, CC SA 1.0 http://creativecommons.org/licenses/sa/1.0/ via Wikimedia Commons; https://commons.wikimedia.org/wiki /File:Pergamonmuseum_Ishtartor_05.jpg

Once Nebuchadnezzar II had expanded and consolidated his empire's borders, he focused on ambitious building projects: completely reconstructing thirteen cities. His primary focus was the city of Babylon, which he transformed into a stunning religious and political center. He restored the Esagila temple of Marduk into an exquisite pilgrimage destination and finished the construction of the towering Etemenanki ziggurat in front of the Esagila.

The Processional Way was a majestic seventy-foot-wide road that began at the gleaming and imposing Ishtar Gate and led through the city to the central temple complex. Fifty-foot walls lined the Processional Way with glistening, blue-glazed bricks and 120 bas-relief images of bulls, dragons, and lions in gold. The Ishtar Gate gleamed in the sun and honored the goddess Ishtar (Inanna). On each side of the cedar and bronze gates, high towers in vibrant blue featured bas-relief depictions of the gods Adad, Ishtar, and Marduk. Marduk's image was a dragon-like creature with a snake head and tail, a scaled lion-like body, and frightful talons on its rear feet.

The dragon-like mušḫuššu represented Marduk.

In addition to constructing stunning cities, Nebuchadnezzar also initiated the excavation of the Royal Canal, or Nebuchadnezzar's Canal, which linked the Euphrates to the Tigris. It was not completed until the end of the Neo-Babylonian era, but it dramatically transformed the region's agriculture.

After ruling the Babylonian Empire for forty-three years, Nebuchadnezzar died in 562 BCE. For unclear reasons, Nebuchadnezzar had chosen one of his younger sons, Amel-Marduk (Evil-Merodach), as the crown prince but later regretted his decision. He believed Amel-Marduk was conspiring against him, disrespectful to the temples, and exploiting the people. When Nebuchadnezzar was absent from Babylon, the nobles declared Amel-Marduk king.

This was odd. Why would the nobles stage a coup against their renowned king and military hero? Was he mentally ill, as Belteshazzar (Daniel) recorded? We will discuss this possibility further in chapter eight. When Nebuchadnezzar returned to Babylon, he locked his son up in the palace dungeon, where Amel-Marduk befriended Judah's King Jehoiachin, whom Nebuchadnezzar had imprisoned thirty-seven years earlier. While Nebuchadnezzar was in the process of appointing a different crown prince, he died suddenly.

When Amel-Marduk ascended the throne, he brought his new friend King Jehoiachin out of prison, and the Judean royal dined at the Babylonian king's table for the rest of his life.[32] Nebuchadnezzar had exiled a number of kings and other royalty to Babylon who retained some sort of status; in the Tanakh, the books of 2 Kings and Jeremiah mention that Amel-Marduk elevated Jehoiachin above the other kings in Babylon.

---

[32] *2 Kings 25,* Tanakh, Book of Malachim II.

In his short reign, inscriptions say that Amel-Marduk "ruled capriciously and had no regard for the laws."[33] He was consumed with worshiping Marduk to the point of neglecting his family and royal duties and offending his courtiers, who refused to obey him. At least, that's what the inscriptions said, but they may have been attempting to justify regicide. After only two years as king, his brother-in-law Neriglissar formed a conspiracy against him, murdered him, and usurped the throne.

Who was Neriglissar? He was one of Nebuchadnezzar's leading generals who had won Nebuchadnezzar's admiration and the hand of the king's daughter. As an astute military leader, he successfully conquered Lydia and Turkey. When King Appuasu of Pirindu assembled a mammoth force to raid Syria, Neriglissar charged out to defend the Babylonian territory. Although Appuasu set an ambush for Neriglissar, the Babylonian king evaded it and trounced Appuasu's army.

After capturing many of Appuasu's men and horses, Neriglissar pursued the Pirindu king for a full day through treacherous mountain passes until he caught up with him and took him prisoner. He then captured Appuasu's royal capital city of Kirsi and burned it down. Following this astounding victory, Neriglissar launched a fleet of ships into the Mediterranean with six thousand troops, defeated the land of Pitusu (probably Crete) in the middle of the sea, flattened the city, and enslaved the people.[34]

After ruling only several years, he fell ill and died. His young son Labashi-Marduk ascended the throne for a brief reign before conspirators beat him to death in another palace coup led by Belshazzar, son of Nabonidus. Nabonidus was surprised to be

---

[33] Frauke Weiershäuser and Jamie Novotny, *The Royal Inscriptions of Amēl-Marduk (561-560 BC), Neriglissar (559-556 BC), and Nabonidus (555-539 BC), Kings of Babylon* (PDF). (Winona Lake: Eisenbrauns, 2020), 1.
[34] *The Chronicle Concerning Year Three of Neriglissar (ABC 6)*, Livius, 2006. https://www.livius.org/sources/content/mesopotamian-chronicles-content/abc-6-neriglissar-chronicle

named king by his son and the other conspirators, as he was not from the Babylonian ruling family. His mother was from the family of Ashurbanipal, the last king of Assyria.

Oddly, after completing a successful military endeavor in Arabia, Nabonidus spent ten of his seventeen years as king in self-imposed exile there. He left his son Belteshazzar to run the empire as regent. In the decade that Nabonidus was away from Babylonia, Cyrus the Great was building his great Persian kingdom in Iran. Nabonidus' neglect of his kingdom left it vulnerable to the imminent threat from the east. Combined with the failure of Nebuchadnezzar's descendants to match his strength and vitality and a series of palace coups, the empire gradually crumbled.

Chapter 7: The Decline and Fall of Babylon

Babylon's decline had begun. Nabonidus had no preparation for ruling an empire. Unrelated to the current Chaldean-Babylonian dynasty, he wasn't even Babylonian; his parents were Assyrian and Aramaean from Harran in Syria. His mother, Adagoppe, daughter of Ashurbanipal, the last Assyrian king, was a priestess to Sin, the moon god. Nabonidus was her only child. Nabonidus referred to his father as "a prince," suggesting he was an Aramaean chieftain or held a prominent position in Harran's government.

Adagoppe's life was upended in 610 BCE when the Babylonians, led by their crown-prince Nebuchadnezzar, conquered Harran and sacked the city. The Babylonians took Adagoppe and her small child Nabonidus as captives; presumably, her husband died in the fighting. As an Assyrian princess, she was treated with the same honor the Babylonians extended to other captured royals. Adagoppe wrote that she introduced Nabonidus to King Nebuchadnezzar II and King Neriglissar, and he was educated and served them in the royal court.[35]

---

[35] Paul-Alain Beaulieu, *Reign of Nabonidus, King of Babylon (556-539 BC)* (New Haven: Yale University Press, 1989), 69.

Nabonidus prays to the moon god Sin, Ishtar, and the sun god on the Harran Stele.
British Museum, CC BY 3.0 https://creativecommons.org/licenses/by/3.0 via Wikimedia Commons; https://commons.wikimedia.org/wiki/File:Nabonidus.jpg

The Babylonian historian Berossus wrote that Nabonidus was a priest of Marduk, so his service to the royals was likely in a religious context. Although he participated in the coup d'état orchestrated by his son Belteshazzar, he never expected to be thrust to the throne. In one of his inscriptions, Nabonidus wryly noted, "In my mind, there was no thought of kingship."[36] Yet, there he was at an advanced age in 556 BCE, wearing the crown, responsible for hundreds of thousands of people of numerous ethnicities and languages spread over thousands of miles.

But Nabonidus' interests lay elsewhere. Intrigued by the ancient histories of Mesopotamia, he wanted to learn more. He is called the world's first archaeologist, as he studied and attempted to interpret the artifacts discovered when the foundations of ancient temples

---

[36] Beaulieu, *Reign of Nabonidus*, 67.

were unearthed to build new ones. He uncovered a statue of Sargon the Great and had it restored, along with Inanna's temple in Agade.[37]

As a priest and the son of a priestess, Nabonidus' primary concern was religion. He rebuilt the temple of the god Sin in Harran, where his mother once served. He renovated Uruk's Eanna temple and changed the order of sacrifices to include offerings that had stopped under King Neriglissar.

Of course, one couldn't be a Mesopotamian king without being a great warrior. Nabonidus excelled in military exploits, leading successful campaigns in Cilicia and Arabia. Mysteriously, after conquering Tayma in Arabia, Nabonidus remained there for about a decade while his son Belteshazzar ran the kingdom as his regent.

Belteshazzar was an inept diplomat, and his citizens were appalled that he failed to celebrate the New Year's religious festival, an ancient Babylonian tradition. Yet, they were even more disgruntled with Nabonidus' long absence and his attempts to force what they considered strange religious reforms.

Why did Nabonidus stay at the isolated desert outpost of Tayma? Why did he conquer the city to begin with, as the Arabians were not a threat to the Babylonians? The answer to the second question was to control the prosperous trade that crossed the deserts. But once he had Tayma under control, he rebuilt the city's walls, erected a new palace for himself, and constructed an elaborate irrigation system: all signs he intended to stay.

Nabonidus deeply wanted to reform the Babylonian religion, but Babylon's priests and his son Belteshazzar staunchly resisted his efforts. Although he had been a priest to Marduk (probably assigned to the position) before becoming king, he desired to elevate Sin over Marduk as the primary god of the Babylonian

---

[37] Beaulieu, *Reign of Nabonidus*, 138.

pantheon. Since Babylon's inception, Marduk had been its chief god, and the Babylonians considered Nabonidus' efforts to supplant Marduk an unholy abomination. Nabonidus wrote in inscriptions that he remained in Tayma because of the "impiety of the Babylonians."[38]

While Nabonidus was in Arabia, he seemed oblivious to the threat of Cyrus the Great, who was building the astounding Persian Empire, surrounding the Babylonian Empire to the east, north, and west. Decades earlier, the Medes had allied with the Persians, sealing their alliance by the marriage of King Cambyses of Persia to Mandane, the daughter of King Astyages of Media and granddaughter of Cyaxares the Great. Cyrus II (Cyrus the Great) was the child of this marriage.

One legend said that when Cyrus was born, King Astyages dreamed that Cyrus would overthrow him one day. He sent his general Harpagus to kill his grandson, but instead, Harpagus gave the baby to a shepherd, who raised him as his own. Ten years later, Cyrus' true identity came to light. Astyages punished Harpagus by killing his son and serving his body to Harpagus at a banquet; however, he permitted Cyrus to return to his biological parents.

At the beginning of Nabonidus' reign, Cyrus was king of Persia, and Astyages ruled the Medes. Cyrus engaged in a power struggle with Astyages and broke off his grandfather's overlordship with the help of General Harpagus, who was eager to avenge his son. Harpagus convinced the Median military to abandon Astyages and join with Cyrus. After Astyages' death, his son Cyaxares II (with the throne name Darius) became the king of the Medes in a subservient position to his nephew Cyrus. When the Medes joined with the Persians, they held power over Bactria (Tajikistan and Uzbekistan), Parthia (northeastern Iran), and the Saka nomads, who roamed the Eurasian Steppe and into what is now China's Xinjiang province.

---

[38] Beaulieu, *Reign of Nabonidus*, 184.

While Nabonidus was in Arabia, not paying attention, the Medes and Persians conquered kingdoms to the north and northwest of Babylonia. They took Lydia in 547 BCE and then shocked the Greek world by defeating the twelve Greek colonies in Ionia, important city-states and trade centers. Cyrus permitted Asia Minor's city-states to continue under self-rule as long as they paid tribute and supplied men for his massive army.

Cyrus put his camels in the front line at the Battle of Thymbra, sending the Lydian horses, which had never seen or smelled camels, into a panic.
https://commons.wikimedia.org/wiki/File:Defeat_of_Croesus_546_BCE.jpg

Cyrus then targeted the Sogdian nomads to the north of Bactria and successfully defeated them. For the next 150 years, they paid a tribute of carnelian, lapis lazuli, and other semiprecious stones. The Medes and Persians also took control of the rest of the Anatolian peninsula (today's western Turkey). Nabonidus' seeming indifference spurred Babylonia's citizens into an increasing malcontent. However, the regent Belshazzar fully understood the Persian peril and reinforced defenses in critical areas.

The Persians' next move was south, down the Mediterranean coastline. The Phoenician cities overlooking the sea, including ancient Tyre, Sidon, Byblos, and Tripoli, did not resist them, aware of Cyrus' track record of mercy toward conquered regions. Cyrus permitted them to carry on as usual with an annual tribute of 350 talents. This was the Persians' first incursion into Babylonian territory, and it finally jolted Nabonidus out of his stupor. Springing into action, Nabonidus returned to Babylon.

Cyrus' next move against the Babylonian Empire was conquering its vassal territory of Elam and its capital Susa, to the southwest of the Babylonian heartland. This impelled Nabonidus to call for the principal statues of the gods and goddesses to be brought from Babylonia's cities and stored in Babylon for safekeeping.[39] Nabonidus then marched north with his troops to defend Sippar and Opis on opposite ends of the Median Wall. Nebuchadnezzar had built the wall to protect against invasions by the Medes, and it stretched from Opis on the Tigris River to Sippar on the Euphrates. Thus, the rivers on both sides and the north wall protected Babylonia.

Cyrus approached with Gubaru (Gobryas), a cunning general whose innovative military tactics were pivotal to Cyrus' invasion of Babylonia. Some scholars believe Gubaru was Cyaxares II, king of the Medes, also known as Darius the Mede. If not, King Darius was also part of the coalition forces. At the end of September 539 BCE, Cyrus' Persian troops and the Medes led by Gubaru approached Opis in the season when the Mesopotamian rivers were at their lowest levels. By overcoming Opis on the eastern shore of the Tigris, Cyrus could ford the river and outflank the Median Wall.

The coalition army of Cyrus and Gubaru launched their assault on Opis, crushing the Babylonian forces, plundering the city, and slaughtering the citizens. Herodotus wrote that Cyrus' engineers diverted the Tigris into several canals, lowering the river level even further, enabling his troops to wade across. Cyrus then divided his army. He led part of his military west to Sippar and sent Gubaru to attack Babylon.

---

[39] *The Chronicle Concerning the Reign of Nabonidus (ABC 7),* Livius, 2020. https://www.livius.org/sources/content/mesopotamian-chronicles-content/abc-7-nabonidus-chronicle/

When Cyrus approached Sippar, the city surrendered on October 10 without a battle. The military leaders defending Sippar were unsupportive of King Nabonidus, who had spent over half his reign outside the country and disrespected their god Marduk. They also may have doubted their ability to defend Sippar, realizing that Cyrus must have already conquered Opis to the east. When Sippar surrendered to Cyrus, Nabonidus fled south.

Oblivious to the catastrophe in the north, the city of Babylon was celebrating the festival of the moon god Sin, which had been on hold all the years Nabonidus was away.[40] They had no inkling that Cyrus had crossed the Tigris, defeated Opis, breached the Median Wall sixty miles north of Babylon, and taken Sippar. With little resistance from the Babylonians between Sippar and Babylon, Gubaru reached Babylon with lightning speed in only two days.

Unaware of the Persian coalition forces rapidly closing in, the co-regent Belshazzar hosted an elaborate dinner for a thousand of his noblemen on the religious holiday. After tasting the wine, Belshazzar commanded that the gold and silver goblets that Nebuchadnezzar had taken from Jerusalem's temple be brought to the palace so his princes, wives, and concubines could drink from them.

Then, suddenly, Belteshazzar looked up. All the color drained from his face, and his legs gave way under him as he saw the disembodied fingers of a human hand inscribing something on the wall! The co-regent shouted for his astrologers and enchanters to read the writing and tell its meaning, but no one could do it. Hearing the clamor, the queen (Nabonidus' wife) hurried into the banquet hall, telling her son not to be so pale and frightened:

"There is a man in your kingdom in whom is the spirit of the holy gods, whom the king Nebuchadnezzar made master of the magicians, astrologers, Chaldeans, and soothsayers.

---

[40] *Reign of Nabonidus (ABC 7).*

Knowledge, understanding, and interpreting of dreams were found in the same Daniel, whom the king named Belteshazzar. Call for Daniel, and he will tell you what the writing means."[41]

By this time, Daniel was an old man in his eighties, brought as a captive to Babylon about sixty-five years earlier. Belshazzar promised to give him a purple robe, a gold chain around his neck, and make him third in the kingdom if he interpreted the writing on the wall. Daniel answered:

"Keep your gifts! Or give them to someone else. You have not honored the God who gives you the breath of life and controls your destiny!

This is what the writing on the wall says: 'mene, mene, tekel, upharsin.'

This is the interpretation: God has numbered the days of your kingdom and ended it. You are weighed in the balances and found wanting. Your kingdom is divided and given to the Medes and Persians."[42]

That night, the Persian forces arrived on the eastern side of the Euphrates, while the Babylonians were drinking and partying in the streets, celebrating the holiday, unaware of their impending doom. Usually, the depth of the Euphrates was about twelve feet deep at that location, but, once again, the Persian engineers diverted the river into a canal, dropping the water level so the Medes and Persians could wade across. They broke through the Enlil Gate, launching a surprise attack on Babylon.

"Thereupon they entered, and of those they met, some were struck down and slain, and others fled into their houses, and some raised the hue and cry, but Gubaru and his friends covered the cry with their shouts, as though they

---

[41] *Daniel 5,* Tanakh: Ketuvim: Book of Daniel.
[42] *Daniel 5,* Tanakh: Ketuvim: Book of Daniel.

were revelers themselves. And thus, making their way by the quickest route, they soon found themselves before the king's palace.

Here the detachment found the gates closed, but the men appointed to attack the guards rushed on them as they lay drinking around a blazing fire and closed with them then and there. As the din grew louder and louder, those within became aware of the tumult, till, the king bidding them see what it meant, some of them opened the gates and ran out. Gubaru and his men, seeing the gates swing wide, darted in, hard on the heels of the others who fled back again, and they chased them at the sword's point into the king's presence.

They found him on his feet with his drawn scimitar. They overwhelmed him by sheer weight of numbers: and not one of his retinue escaped; they were all cut down, some flying, others snatching up anything to serve as a shield and defending themselves as best they could."[43]

The "king" killed by Gubaru's men was the regent Belshazzar, not his father King Nabonidus, according to Belteshazzar (Daniel), an eyewitness to the events: "That very night Belshazzar was killed, and Darius the Mede took over the kingdom at the age of sixty-two."[44]

The Babylonian historian Berossus said Darius the Mede was the Median king Cyaxares II, Cyrus' uncle. Gubaru may have been the same person, but more likely, he was of lesser status. Daniel called Darius a king, saying he divided the realm into 120 provinces and appointed satraps (governors); this implies Darius ruled over

---

[43] Xenophon, *Cyropaedia: The Education of Cyrus,* trans. Henry Graham Dakyns. (Project Gutenberg E-book). https://www.gutenberg.org/files/2085/2085-h/2085-h.htm

[44] *Daniel 5,* Tanakh: Ketuvim: Book of Daniel.

the whole empire temporarily, not just Babylonia.[45] The *Nabonidus Chronicle* says Gubaru appointed the district officers of Babylonia as the appointed satrap of Babylonia.[46] Cyrus may have designated his uncle, King Darius of the Medes, as regent over the empire while he finished consolidating the Levant.

What happened to Nabonidus? The *Nabonidus Chronicle (ABC 7)* recorded that Nabonidus initially fled following Sippar's surrender to Cyrus, but the Persians captured him after Cyrus conquered Babylon. Cyrus treated him kindly and sent him to live in Carmania (Iran).[47]

Cyrus arrived with great fanfare about two weeks later. Persian inscriptions said the people of Babylon threw open the gates and welcomed Cyrus as their deliverer with peace, joy, and jubilation. This propaganda likely whitewashed the invasion; however, the Babylonians were clearly unhappy with their absentee king and his despotic regent. Cyrus' reputation of considerate treatment of submissive conquered cities preceded him, and few Babylonians resisted the Persian takeover.

The Medes and Persians treated the religious sites and temples with the utmost respect and encouraged the priests to continue the worship rituals. Cyrus offered the Magi the first pick of the spoils of war to consecrate to the gods. He returned all the cult images of the Babylonian deities that Nabonidus had gathered into Babylon and publicly worshiped Marduk, endearing himself to the Babylonians.

Cyrus took the title "King of Babylon, Sumer, and Akkad. King of the four corners of the earth." Once he consolidated Mesopotamia under his rule, he swiftly conquered northern Arabia, Israel, and Syria. Cyrus reversed the population-relocation program

---

[45] *Daniel 6.*

[46] *Reign of Nabonidus (ABC 7).*

[47] Beaulieu, *Reign of Nabonidus,* 231.

the Babylonians and Assyrians used against rebel provinces. He permitted the Jews and other exiles to return home in the first year of his reign, although Daniel and many others remained in Babylonia in leadership positions. Cyrus ordered the rebuilding of Jerusalem's temple:

> "Concerning the house of God at Jerusalem, let the temple, where sacrifices are offered, be rebuilt. Let its foundations be retained, its height being sixty cubits and its width sixty cubits, with three layers of huge stones and one layer of timbers. And let the cost be paid from the royal treasury. Also, let the gold and silver utensils of the house of God, which Nebuchadnezzar took from the temple in Jerusalem and brought to Babylon, be returned and brought to their places in the temple in Jerusalem; you shall put them in the house of God."[48]

Cyrus' vast Achaemenid Empire reached from Asia Minor to the Indus River by the end of his life. He won the hearts of his new subjects through extraordinary humanity and respect for their cultures. He governed Babylonia and his other vast territories through a centralized administration, with a governor (satrap) over each province. Under Persian rule, Babylon became a center of scientific and mathematic knowledge. A year before he died in 530 BCE, Cyrus appointed his son Cambyses II as Babylon's king, while he continued as the empire's king.

---

[48] *Ezra 6.* Tanakh: Ketuvim, Book of Ezra.

A Greek painting of Darius the Great.
Carlo Raso, CC BY-SA 2.0 <https://creativecommons.org/licenses/by-sa/2.0>, via Wikimedia Commons, https://commons.wikimedia.org/w/index.php?curid=74758953

After the short reigns of Cyrus' sons, Darius I (the Great) seized control of the Persian Empire. Taking advantage of the chaos, Babylonia declared independence in 521 BCE under King Nebuchadnezzar III, who ruled for about a year. Darius led an enormous army against Babylon, where the citizens jeered him from the walls, "You'll capture Babylon when mules have foals!" Typically, mules are sterile, but a mule gave birth after an unsuccessful twenty-month siege of Babylon! This miraculous event galvanized the Persians to take Babylon successfully. Darius did not show the Babylonians the mercy they had received under Cyrus. He impaled three thousand leading citizens and pulled down the city's massive gates and defenses.[49]

Over the next two centuries, as Persia's vassal kingdom, Babylonia declined. High taxes and warfare led to the neglect of the elegant temples and canal systems necessary for adequate agriculture. Two other rebellions sprung up, but Persia quickly suppressed the renegades. When Alexander the Great conquered the Persian Empire in 331 BCE, Babylon became his home and center of operations when he wasn't leading military expeditions. He adopted the Babylonian dress, reverenced the temples, and the city flourished in his brief stay. He planned to restore Babylon's ziggurat but unexpectedly died in Babylon before he could see it through.

Babylon maintained its urban life through two centuries of warfare between Alexander's successors, but it was no longer an administrative or economic hub. Alexandria in Egypt took over as the center of science and mathematics for the known world. Babylon's Esagila temple remained a religious center and pilgrimage destination, but gradually, Babylon deteriorated. When the Muslims invaded Babylonia in the mid-seventh century CE, Babylon had dwindled to only a village. The ruins of the once majestic city were a source of bricks for construction elsewhere.

---

[49] Herodotus, *Capture of Babylon.* Livius. https://www.livius.org/articles/person/darius-the-great/sources/capture-of-babylon-herodotus

Chapter 8: Babylonian Society and Famous Rulers

Babylonia was a majestic empire, pivotal to ancient Middle Eastern history, but history is always the story of people. From those who lived in palaces to the commoners of shops and farms, Babylonia's people were consequential to its three-time rise and fall. We've already discussed the exploits of many of its leaders, but what about its ordinary citizens? What was their social structure, and how did they live their everyday lives? How did the Babylonians develop military technology? What more can we learn about their famous leaders? Aside from great conquests, what were they like as people?

Hammurabi's law code, which we will discuss more extensively in chapter nine, gives a fascinating insight into Babylonian family life and women's legal status.[50] For instance, if a wife were caught in adultery, she and her lover would be drowned in the river unless her husband pardoned her. If someone accused a woman of adultery, but with no proof, she could "jump into the river": if she drowned, she was guilty, but if she survived, she was innocent.

---

[50] *The Code of Hammurabi*, trans. L.W. King (The Avalon Project: Documents in Law, History, and Diplomacy. Yale Law School: Lillian Goldman Law Library). https://avalon.law.yale.edu/ancient/hamframe.asp

If a man violated a virgin girl betrothed to another man, the rapist would receive the death penalty, but the girl would be considered innocent. If a man abandoned his wife and she moved in with another man, the husband could not reclaim his wife if he returned.

This bas-relief of a man and woman dates to the Old Babylonian era.
Osama Shukir Muhammed Amin FRCP(Glasg), CC BY-SA 4.0
https://creativecommons.org/licenses/by-sa/4.0 via Wikimedia Commons;
https://commons.wikimedia.org/wiki/File:Man_and_woman,_Old-
Babylonian_fired_clay_plaque_from_Southern_Mesopotamia,_Iraq.jpg

When a woman married, her husband paid a "bride price" to her father, and her father gave her a dowry. Her husband had no claim to the dowry for his own use: it was for her children. If a man separated from the mother of his children, he had to return her dowry and give her the benefit of part of his field and garden to support the children. Once their children grew up, he had to provide her with a payment, and then she could marry "the man of her heart." If a couple had no children, the husband simply needed to return her dowry to divorce her. The only time a man could divorce his wife without returning her dowry was if she were a substandard wife, running up debts and neglecting her husband and home.

A man could take a second wife if his first wife could not conceive, but the first wife would hold higher status over the second. If a wife became chronically ill, the husband could take a second wife, but he had to permit his first wife to live in his home and care for her as long as she lived. She could leave if she wanted to, but he had to return her dowry. A man could have a wife and also have sexual relations with a maidservant in his home. If he acknowledged the maid's children as his own, both his legitimate sons and his sons by the maid would receive equal portions of his estate. A man was expected to provide a dowry and arrange a marriage for his daughter by a concubine.

What if a man had several sons and arranged marriages for them (paying their bride prices) but died before negotiating a union for the youngest son? In that case, the older brothers had to set aside money for their younger brother's bride price before dividing up the property among them; they also had to arrange a marriage for their brother.

The Babylonian social hierarchy had five principal layers: nobility, middle class, landowning farmers, tenant farmers, and enslaved people. The elite *awilum* or *mar bane* (nobility and upper class) were "freemen" of the royal family, chief administrators, high-ranking military, high-ranking priests and priestesses (often members of the royal family), and owners of large estates.

The term *muškenum* in Hammurabi's code appeared to refer to anyone in the middle status between the *awilum* elite class and the *wardum*, or slaves. This middle class comprised scribes, lower-ranking priests and priestesses, merchants, skilled artisans, and farmers. The regular farmers were owners of smaller plots, and they often performed double duty: serving in the lower military ranks and coming home in time for planting and harvesting. Tenant farmers worked the large estates' fields. The landowner usually provided housing, and the tenant's harvest would be split three ways: part for taxes, part for the landowner, and part for the tenant farmer.

Slaves (*wardum*) ranked lowest in Babylonian society, and a person could become enslaved in two ways. One was being captured in war, but usually, the Babylonians only brought back scribes and highly-skilled artisans. If a man had a debt he could not pay, he could sell himself, his wife, or his children into slavery. They would work for three years for the person who bought them and go free in the fourth year.

Giving shelter to a runaway slave meant the death penalty, but if a man returned a runaway slave to his owner, the owner had to pay two shekels. If an enslaved man married a free woman, their children would be free. If a slave married to a free woman later died, she had to give half her dowry and any accumulated wealth from the marriage to her husband's owner. If an enslaved person was accidentally killed or seriously injured, the penalty for the offender was less than for a free person.

Throughout its history, trade was intrinsic to the Babylonian economy. The population relocations of rebellious conquered people into Babylonia, first by the Assyrians and later by Nebuchadnezzar II, created ethnic groups of Babylonians with solid ties to their lands of origin. They were integrated into the social and commercial Babylonian milieu but maintained contact with their homelands, with the language knowledge and valuable contacts intrinsic to trade.

Even before the massive population shifts, the Mesopotamian people traded with the Eastern Mediterranean, Armenia, Elam, and points along the Persian Gulf. The fertile Mesopotamian river system provided surplus food, which the Babylonians traded for wood, metal, and luxuries like precious and semiprecious stones, dyes, and incense. The courtyards of the Babylonian temples served as a marketplace, and the priests and priestesses were among the chief buyers of luxury items for adorning the temples.

Thousands of clay tablets with cuneiform script and the Aramaic alphabet illustrate the Babylonians' literacy level. Written communication included letters, hymns, prayers, inscriptions on monuments, sales records and inventory, history annals, law codes, property transactions, and legal documents. A portion of Babylon's society knew how to read and write, and everyone else hired scribes. Young people from wealthier families were tutored at home or attended privately-run schools, often in the temples.

In the Neo-Babylonian Empire, scribes had to learn both cuneiform and Aramaic script and be fluent in several languages. They practiced by copying older tablets and transcribing their teachers' dictations. One scribal duty was preserving the ancient literature of the Sumerians, Akkadians, Assyrians, and earlier Babylonians; the scribes would translate and copy these history annals, myths, prayers, and other literature.

What language did the Babylonians speak? The Akkadian, Assyrian, Babylonian, Arabic, and Hebrew languages were all from the Semitic language family. However, the written Assyrian and Babylonian languages were so close to Akkadian that most linguists classify them as dialects of Akkadian, although the spoken languages may have been more distinct. Throughout Babylonia's history, the people would have spoken Babylonian-Akkadian; they probably also spoke Sumerian in the First Babylonian dynasty. We don't know what language the Kassite-era Babylonians spoke, but they wrote in the Sumerian and Akkadian languages.

Aramaic, another Semitic language initially spoken in Syria, gradually took precedence. The Neo-Assyrians used Aramaic as their second official language, and it eventually replaced Akkadian, becoming the Neo-Babylonian Empire's standard spoken and written language. The Aramaic alphabet was far easier to read and write than the ancient cuneiform, which required a distinctive character for every word. One had to memorize at least six hundred characters for basic literacy in cuneiform, but written Aramaic used only twenty-two letters, all consonants.

The Chaldean King Marduk-apla-iddina (722–710 BCE) and his attendant wear ankle-length skirts with long sashes. The king is wearing a conical hat.
https://commons.wikimedia.org/wiki/File:Marduk-apla-iddina_II.jpg

What did the Babylonians wear? Both men and women wore long tunics or skirts that often fell in tiers. Sometimes, a gown would come up over one shoulder like a toga and be trimmed with fringe.

In summer or when doing heavy work, men would wear a simple knee-length skirt and go bare-chested. Men often wore conical or bowl-shaped hats and long beards, elaborately braided or curled if they were upper-class. They wore their hair down to their shoulders, also often braided or curled.

Women also wore curled or braided shoulder-length hair. The tops of their tunics covered their breasts and sometimes were bandeau-style, with one or both shoulders bare but more often with a modest, rounded neckline. Their gowns might have short or long sleeves or be sleeveless. Both men and women wore earrings, headbands, bracelets, and necklaces of gold and precious metals.

This woman holding a baby from the Old Babylonian period wears a full-length, tiered tunic and elaborately-braided shoulder-length hair.
Photo modified: zoomed-in. Credit: Osama Shukir Muhammed Amin FRCP(Glasg), CC BY-SA 4.0 https://creativecommons.org/licenses/by-sa/4.0 via Wikimedia Commons; https://commons.wikimedia.org/wiki/File:Old-Babylonian_plaque_of_a_standing_woman_holding_her_child,_from_Southern_Mesopotamia,_Iraq.jpg

Babylonia's military assimilated some of the tactics used by the Sumerians, Akkadians, and Assyrians but often added its own twists. Generally speaking, Babylonia's kings and military commanders were not as cruel as some of the notorious Assyrian kings and Akkad's King Rimush. They usually did not torture conquered or rebellious populations or wipe out large populations. The exception was when they allied with the Scythians, Medes, and Parthians for Assyria's final defeat.

Interestingly, on two occasions when they allied with these tribes, they arrived late for the battle, after their allies had broken the city's defenses and were plundering the temples and palaces. Perhaps the Babylonians were slow to muster their troops. But maybe they were canny: why endanger their own men and horses when their partners were eager to do the dangerous part of eliminating their enemies?

A common tactic used by the Babylonian military was diverting rivers into existing irrigation canals or new canals they dug themselves. This enabled them to cross even large rivers like the Tigris and Euphrates. A well-used strategy for conquering a city was to flood it in two ways: damming and suddenly releasing the river's water or diverting the river to flow into the city. On more than one occasion, they defended themselves against invading Assyrians by redirecting the river and canal system to form a lake around their own forces!

Aside from their innovative military tactics, what more can we know about Babylonia's famous rulers? Hammurabi, the famous conqueror of the Old Babylonian Empire, wrote one of the world's earliest and most complex law codes, but he also engaged in outstanding building projects that put Babylon on the map. He transformed Babylon by promoting the god Marduk and constructing majestic temples, palaces, and city walls. What was once a humble and unremarkable small town grew into a breathtaking metropolis that usurped Nippur's position as

Mesopotamia's "holy city" and became the political capital of Sumer and Akkad.

Hammurabi ruled from 1792 to 1750 BCE (middle chronology).
Mbmrock, CC BY-SA 4.0 https://creativecommons.org/licenses/by-sa/4.0 via Wikimedia Commons; https://commons.wikimedia.org/wiki/ File:(Mesopotamia)_Hammurabi.jpg

Hammurabi's promotion of Marduk from an obscure city god to the supreme deity of the pantheon proved problematic for the god: he was constantly being stolen. That is, his cult image (idol) was stolen, but the Mesopotamians believed their gods inhabited the statues. If someone removed a god's cult image from the city, it meant the god had left the city, which would bring all sorts of misfortune. Even though he was a god, Marduk couldn't get back on his own. He had to wait for months or even years before someone brought him back to Babylon.

Rescuing Marduk was one of the things for which King Nebuchadnezzar I was famous. Although not as well-known as his Neo-Babylonian namesake Nebuchadnezzar II, the first Nebuchadnezzar was a king of Isin who conquered and ruled Babylon from 1121 to 1100 BCE. His rescue of Marduk, stolen earlier by the Elamites, is immortalized in the *Epic of Nabu-kudurri-uṣur I*.[51] The *Marduk Prophecy* also tells of Marduk's journeys to different points outside Babylon.[52] Although Marduk enjoyed his stay with the Hittites and Assyrians, he found Elam distasteful. He prophesied his return to Babylon through a zealous king who would avenge the sacking of Babylon and Marduk's theft, and that king turned out to be Nebuchadnezzar I.

Nabopolassar, the "Avenger of Akkad," is known chiefly for crushing Assyria for all time and initiating the Neo-Babylonian Empire in 626 BCE. But the Babylonians and even the Greeks remembered Nabopolassar for his piety, fair-mindedness, and integrity. He rose to power from obscurity, crediting Marduk's patronage and the support of Babylonia's priests and noblemen. The Babylonians, Hellenists, and even the Jewish historian Josephus portrayed him as a just king who deeply reverenced Marduk. The Babylonians and Nabopolassar himself concluded that his devoutness elevated him to kingship, enabling him to liberate Babylonia and conquer the Assyrians when previous kings had failed:

---

[51] *Cuneiform Texts from Babylonian Tablets in the British Museum: Part XIII* (Piccadilly: Longmans and Co., 1901), 54.
https://www.yumpu.com/en/document/read/18926135/babylonian-tablets-c
[52] Joshua J. Mark, "The Marduk Prophecy," *World History Encyclopedia* (2016).
https://www.worldhistory.org/article/990/the-marduk-prophecy

"Šazu perceived my intentions, and he placed me, the insignificant one who was not even noticed among the people, in the highest position in my native country. He called me to the lordship over land and people."[53]

Nabopolassar's son Nebuchadnezzar II was Neo-Babylonia's shining star, yet he did not always display his father's humility. Daniel's account in the Tanakh tells how he paid the price for his pride and impiety:

"One night, I had a dream that terrified me. When all the magicians, enchanters, astrologers, and fortune-tellers came in, I told them the dream, but they could not tell me what it meant. At last, Daniel came in before me, and I told him the dream. (He was named Belteshazzar after my god, and the spirit of the holy gods is in him.)"[54]

Nebuchadnezzar told Belteshazzar his dream of a great tree reaching to heaven, loaded with fruit for the entire world and providing shade and protection to all. But then he heard a voice from heaven saying to cut down the tree but leave the stump. When Belteshazzar heard Nebuchadnezzar's dream, he was horror-stricken:

"I wish the events foreshadowed in this dream would happen to your enemies, my lord, and not to you! That tree, Your Majesty, is you. You have grown strong, and your greatness reaches up to heaven and your rule to the ends of the earth.

This is what the dream means, Your Majesty, and what the Most High has declared will happen to my lord the king. You will be driven from human society and live in the fields

---

[53] Rocío Da Riva, "The Figure of Nabopolassar in Late Achaemenid and Hellenistic Historiographic Tradition: BM 34793 and CUA 90," *Journal of Near Eastern Studies* 76, no.1. https://www.journals.uchicago.edu/doi/full/10.1086/690464

[54] *Daniel 4.* Tanakh, Navi, Book of Daniel.

with the wild animals. You will eat grass like a cow, and you will be drenched with the dew of heaven.

Seven periods of time will pass while you live this way until you learn that the Most High rules over the kingdoms of the world and gives them to anyone he chooses. But the stump and tree roots were left in the ground, and this means that you will receive your kingdom back again when you have learned that heaven rules."[55]

William Blake's relief etching depicts Nebuchadnezzar's madness as told by Daniel.
https://commons.wikimedia.org/wiki/File:William_Blake_-_Nebuchadnezzar_(Tate_Britain).jpg

The dream came true twelve months later, as Nebuchadnezzar was pridefully gazing at Babylon from the roof of his palace, boasting of his power, the beautiful city he had built, and his majestic splendor. He lost his sanity and crawled about in the fields, eating grass like an animal "until his hair was as long as eagles' feathers and his nails were like birds' claws." Finally, when his reason returned, Nebuchadnezzar acknowledged and praised God, who restored him as head of the kingdom.

---

[55] *Daniel 4,* Tanakh, Navi, Book of Daniel.

Many scholars dismiss Belteshazzar's account in the *Tanakh* due to the lack of other Babylonian records corroborating Nebuchadnezzar's madness or a seven-month (or seven-year) period of absence from Babylon. Some historians believe the story actually refers to Nabonidus, the last king of the Neo-Babylonians, who spent ten years in exile in Tayma, Arabia. The *Verse Account of Nabonidus* alludes to mental illness.[56] The *Prayer of Nabonidus*, found in the Dead Sea Scrolls, stated, "I was afflicted for seven years...and an exorcist pardoned my sins. He was a Jew from among the children of the exile of Judah."[57]

Belteshazzar (Daniel) was an exile from Judah, he was alive in Nabonidus' day, and he may have been the one who ministered to Nabonidus. However, a badly-damaged cuneiform text in the British Museum implies Nebuchadnezzar experienced a mental break. He no longer valued his life, gave confusing orders, neglected his children and family, and lost interest in the Esagila temple and Babylon's affairs.

The text said that the Babylonians gave "bad counsel" to Evil-Merodach (Amel-Marduk, Nebuchadnezzar's son).[58] Nebuchadnezzar's son Nabû-šuma-ukīn (believed to be Amel-Marduk) took part in a coup against Nebuchadnezzar and was thrown into prison.[59] Why would his son and nobles seek to supplant Nebuchadnezzar? Where was Nebuchadnezzar while this was happening? What destabilized Babylon in this latter part of Nebuchadnezzar's reign? Only four inscriptions have survived that document Nebuchadnezzar's activities in this period, compared to over fifty in his first ten years.

[56] *Verse Account of Nabonidus*, trans A. Leo Oppenheim. Livius. https://www.livius.org/sources/content/anet/verse-account-of-nabonidus/
[57] *Prayer of Nabonidus (4Q242)*. Livius. https://www.livius.org/sources/content/dss/4q242-prayer-of-nabonidus/
[58] A. K. Grayson, *Babylonian Historical-Literary Texts: Toronto Semitic Texts and Studies, 3* (Toronto: University of Toronto Press, 1975), 87-92.
[59] Irving Finkel, "The Lament of Nabû-šuma-ukîn." in *Focus Mesopotamischer Geschichte, Wiege früher Gelehrtsamkeit, Mythos in der Moderne.* (Saaerbrücken, 1999), 323-341.

If nothing else, Babylonia's well-known kings were complex, multifaceted individuals who struggled with humility and mental soundness. They were propelled to greatness by their ability to think differently and innovatively. Sometimes, they experienced dramatic successes; other times, people thought they were experiencing mental breaks, and perhaps some were. When a king achieved astounding triumphs, and everyone dropped to the floor in worship when he entered the room, staying grounded in reality would be challenging.

Chapter 9: Culture and Innovation

The Babylonian powerhouse generated astounding advances in the arts, sciences, and law. Their libraries held impressive literature collections from throughout the Middle East, and their mosaics and distinctive architecture were unparalleled. They made unimaginable leaps in the knowledge of medicine, mathematics, astronomy, and concepts of time. Their legal codes served as prototypes for generations to come.

Babylonia hosted the world's first known libraries. However, the Assyrians quickly imitated their southern neighbors, with copies of Babylonian literature stored in Ashurbanipal's palace library in Nineveh. One impressive Babylonian collection of seventy tablets on astronomy and astrology dates to 2000 BCE and discusses the movements of comets, the north star (Polaris), and Venus. Other noteworthy collections included mathematical formulas, such as cube roots. The libraries contained fascinating historical chronicles and famous literature: poems, hymns, and epic tales.

Excavation of a temple at Sippar uncovered fifty thousand clay tablets, mostly cataloging business transactions, administrative affairs, and private correspondence. However, it also included a respectable literary collection with a narrative of the Great Flood and vital religious texts, including incantations, hymns, and prayers. Evidence from the documents showed that the temple had a school that taught reading, writing, and mathematics. Archaeologists uncovered similar collections in a temple in Nippur.

One of the most acclaimed Babylonian literary works, and possibly the world's oldest, is the *Epic of Gilgamesh*. The oldest full copy of the epic dates to around 1800 BCE, but five Sumerian poems from about 2100 BCE tell part of the story, and it likely had an oral history that went back even further. The captivating epic is about King Gilgamesh, a real-life king of Uruk (based on ancient inscriptions and the *Sumerian King List*), yet the story contains fantastical elements.

Gilgamesh was part human and part divine in the legend, with unmatched strength and beauty. Yet, he had a dark side: he claimed the "right of the first night," forcing himself on Uruk's virgin brides on their wedding day. When Uruk's people complained of this injustice to the gods, the gods created Enkidu, a hairy wild man as strong as Gilgamesh. He roamed the plains with the wild herds, eating grass.

A trapper saw Enkidu shoving his way through the animals at the watering hole. Frightened, he hurried home to tell his father about the wild man; no doubt he was the one who had been setting the animals free from his traps! His father told him to get Shamhat, the prostitute, to tame this feral creature. Then they could use him as their champion against their hated king Gilgamesh.

Shamhat agreed to the plan and went out to the watering hole; when Enkidu showed up, she opened her gown. One look at Shamhat's beautiful figure and Enkidu forgot everything but having sexual relations with her for the next seven days. But now, his animal friends ran away when they saw him. Shamhat taught Enkidu how to eat human food, and he especially enjoyed his first rounds of beer!

Shamhat invited Enkidu to come with her to Uruk, telling him they needed help overthrowing their wicked king. She told him a wedding was taking place that night, and King Gilgamesh would force himself on the bride. Enkidu marched into Uruk to defend the bride and stationed himself outside her door, refusing to let Gilgamesh in. The two men lunged at each other and brawled ferociously, but they were equally strong, and neither could overcome the other. They stepped back, exhausted, looked at each other, then kissed and became friends.

They grew so excited about what they could do with their combined strength that they forgot all about the bride and plotted to kill the Humbaba monster, guardian of Lebanon's cedar forest. They quickly marched toward Lebanon, and when they arrived, Humbaba sneered at them, "I will feed your bodies to the shrieking vultures!"

But the two mighty men killed Humbaba, cutting off his head. They built a raft and sailed back to Uruk, but the goddess Ishtar saw Gilgamesh bathing just before he arrived in Uruk. When he shook out his long curls, she was stirred to lust and called out, "Gilgamesh! Come, be my husband!"

Gilgamesh laughed, "Where are all your other bridegrooms? Where's Tammuz, your shepherd? You send him to Hades for half of every year!"

Infuriated, Ishtar flew up to her father Anu in heaven. "Father! Gilgamesh mocked me repeatedly! Give me the Bull of Heaven, or I'll rip open the gates of the underworld, and the zombies will come out to eat the living people!"

Anu gave her the Bull of Heaven, and Ishtar led it to Uruk. The Bull snorted, the ground opened, and one hundred men fell into an abyss. A second time, the Bull snorted, and two hundred men fell into a second hole. The third time the Bull snorted, Enkidu began to fall but quickly grabbed the Bull's horns. "Quick, Gilgamesh! Stab the Bull!"

When Ishtar saw her Bull was dead, she screeched curses from Uruk's wall, but Enkidu flung the Bull's hindquarter at her. The horrified gods conferred and determined they had to execute one of the men; they were getting out of control and killing the divine animals! Although Gilgamesh had been the one to kill both Humbaba and the Bull of Heaven, the gods sentenced Enkidu to death.

Gilgamesh kills the Bull of Heaven.
Royal Museums of Art and History, Public domain, via Wikimedia Commons; https://en.wikipedia.org/wiki/Bull_of_Heaven#/media/File:O.1054_color.jpg

With tears flowing, Gilgamesh mourned Enkidu for six days and seven nights, not letting anyone bury his friend until a maggot fell out of Enkidu's nose. Horrified, Gilgamesh considered his own mortality: he would be lying dead like Enkidu one day! He set off to find Utnapishtim, who had built the ark to save people and animals from the Great Flood. Utnapishtim was still alive after all these centuries, and Gilgamesh wanted to learn the key to immortality.

Gilgamesh hiked to the highest peak, Mount Mashu, then tunneled through twelve terrifying leagues of utter darkness. He emerged into brilliant light and sailed through the Waters of Death until he reached Utnapishtim's land. "Why do you look so devastated?" the patriarch asked.

"How could I not despair?" Gilgamesh asked. "My best friend died! I can't be silent. Won't I meet the same fate? I must know, how did you discover immortality?"

Utnapishtim told his story, "When Anu planned to flood the whole earth, the god Ea spoke to me through the wall of my reed house. He told me to build a boat and bring all the animals inside. After I built the boat and covered it with bitumen, the rain started falling. It rained for six days and seven nights, covering the people and even the mountains. Finally, the wind and rain stopped, and the ark rested on Mount Nimush.

"After seven days, I released a dove, who flew around but came back to me, unable to find a place to land. Later, I released a swallow, but it came back. Finally, I released a raven, and it flew away, never to return. I let the animals out of the ark and sacrificed a sheep to the gods. At that point, the god Enlil gifted my wife and me with immortality."

Utnapishtim told Gilgamesh about a unique plant growing under the sea that gave eternal life. Tying rocks to his feet, Gilgamesh sank into the sea, discovered the magical plant, cut it, then untied the stones and swam up to the surface. But traveling home with the plant of eternity, he stopped to bathe in a spring, and a snake stole his plant! Gilgamesh collapsed to the ground, weeping. Finally, he traveled home to Uruk, realizing that his legacy would continue through his city even though he would die.

In addition to its remarkable literature, the Neo-Babylonian Empire sparked a cultural renaissance of exquisite art and stunning architecture, featuring majestic temples with brightly-colored walls. The Greek historian Herodotus said Babylon was the most breathtaking city of its day, with city walls so wide that chariots could ride on top. The three palaces and temples gleamed with bricks glazed in yellow and blue, adorned with bright mosaics of lions, dragons, and horses.

Towering over the rest of the city stood the ninety-one-meter high Etemenanki ziggurat, the "foundation of heaven on earth." The Mesopotamian ziggurats were tall and massive terraced structures that were part of their cities' temple complexes. The Etemenanki had a shrine to Marduk at its top and stood next to the Esagila temple. The Etemenanki would have been one of the world's highest structures in its day, with its terraced sides appearing as steps up to heaven.

Was the Etemenanki ziggurat the Tower of Babel?
Александр Михальчук, CC BY-SA 4.0 https://creativecommons.org/licenses/by-sa/4.0 via Wikimedia Commons; https://commons.wikimedia.org/wiki/ File:The_Tower_of_Babel_Alexander_Mikhalchyk.jpg

The Amorites probably built the original ziggurat during the Old Babylonian Period (1894–1595 BCE), when Babylon was likely the largest city in the world. Like other Mesopotamian ziggurats, it was probably remodeled and rebuilt several times over the centuries. The Assyrian king Sennacherib bragged of destroying it in 689 BCE. Nebuchadnezzar II completed the final structure after forty-three years of work during the Neo-Babylonian Empire when

Babylon was likely once again the world's largest city. Nebuchadnezzar II reported that he and two of his sons even took part in the construction project (at least ritually):

"I rolled up my garment, my kingly robe, and carried on my head bricks and earth. I had soil-baskets made of gold and silver and made Nebuchadnezzar, my firstborn son, beloved of my heart, carry alongside my workmen earth mixed with wine, oil, and resin chips. I made Nabûsumilisir, his brother, a boy, issue of my body, my darling younger son, take up mattock and spade. I burdened him with a soil-basket of gold and silver and bestowed him on my lord Marduk as a gift. I constructed the building, the replica of E-Sarra, in joy and jubilation and raised its top as high as a mountain."[60]

Many scholars believe the earlier Etemenanki ziggurat was the Tower of Babel, which the Torah said was built following the Great Flood:

"As the people migrated to the east, they found a plain in the land of Shinar (Babylonia) and settled there. They said to each other, 'Let's make bricks and harden them with fire.'

Then they said, 'Come, let's build a great city for ourselves with a tower that reaches into the sky. This will make us famous and keep us from being scattered all over the world.'

But the LORD came down to look at the city and the tower the people were building. 'Look!' he said. 'The people are united, and they all speak the same language. After this, nothing they set out to do will be impossible for them! Come, let's go down and confuse the people with

---

[60] Andrew George, "The Tower of Babel: Archaeology, History and Cuneiform Texts," *Archiv für Orientforschung* 51 (2005/2006): 75–95.
https://eprints.soas.ac.uk/3858/2/TowerOfBabel.AfO.pdf

different languages. Then they won't be able to understand each other.'

In that way, the LORD scattered them all over the world, and they stopped building the city. That is why the city was called Babel because that is where the LORD confused the people with different languages. In this way, he scattered them all over the world."[61]

Nebuchadnezzar II built not only the Etemenanki ziggurat but also the Hanging Gardens of Babylon. Philo of Byzantium lauded the gardens in an ancient Greek tour guide, *On the Seven Wonders*, written in 225 BCE. Other historians who spoke of seeing the Hanging Gardens included Callimachus of Cyrene (310-340 BCE), Berossus of Babylon (third century BCE), Antipater of Sidon (second century BCE), and Diodorus Siculus (first century BCE).

They described the gardens as ingeniously laid out on a trellis of reeds over palm tree beams supported by stone columns. All sorts of flowers and trees grew high in the air in ascending tiers and were irrigated by a pump system bringing water up from the river. Although archaeologists haven't yet discovered the remains of the gardens, the literary evidence with detailed descriptions advocates for the garden's existence, not only in the Neo-Babylonian era but also in the subsequent Persian era.

---

[61] *Genesis 11,* Tanakh: Torah: Book of Bereishit.

Berossus wrote that Nebuchadnezzar II built Babylon's Hanging Gardens to please his wife Amytis, who missed the mountains of her Iranian homeland. *https://commons.wikimedia.org/wiki/File:Hanging_Gardens_of_Babylon_by_Ferdina nd_Knab_(1886).png*

Babylonians matched their artistic genius with astonishing advances in medicine, astronomy, and mathematics. The Babylonians produced medical texts as early as the original Amorite dynasty (1894–1595 BCE). Esagil-kin-apli, the chief scholar of king Adad-apla-iddina (1067–1046 BCE), wrote the forty-tablet *Sakikkū* or the *Diagnostic Handbook*, introducing concepts of diagnosis, prognosis, etiology, therapy, and prescriptions. A Babylonian pharmacy inventoried about five hundred medicines around 1000 BCE.

The *Diagnostic Handbook* took a supernatural approach to medicine, including omens a physician might encounter. He recorded symptoms and treatment of neurological issues believed to be associated with demonic forces requiring exorcism, such as basal ganglia disorders, brain tumors and trauma, epilepsy, motor impairments, tetanus, and stroke. Esagil-kin-apli also wrote on skin problems, fever, gynecological care, pregnancy, childbirth, and childhood illnesses.

Physicians refined their surgery techniques and knowledge of wound care throughout Babylonian history. Although they didn't have hospitals for multiple patients, doctors did treat patients in smaller clinics, with beds for those requiring overnight care. Surgeries included relieving pleural effusion in the lungs, setting bones, excising wounds, draining abscesses, and castrating boys who were to become eunuchs. Their instruments included scalpels and bronze lancets.

Doctors had specific guidelines in *The Code of Hammurabi*. They had to charge fees on a sliding scale: the highest for those of the noble class, one-half the amount for the middle class, and one-fifth the amount for enslaved people. If a doctor's malpractice resulted in a patient's death, his hands would be chopped off unless the dead person were a slave. In that case, the physician had to give the owner the purchase price for a replacement slave.

From their earliest history, Babylonians were keenly interested in astronomy and time. They recorded the length of daylight on each day of the solar year and employed mathematics to study the earth's rotation. They developed our twelve-month calendar with each month having four seven-day weeks, except they didn't add in the extra days as we do. They occasionally added a thirteenth month to keep their lunar calendar in sync with the solar-determined seasons. Each day had twelve *kaspus* (two hours) marking each time the sun traveled thirty degrees.

For the Babylonians, astronomy and astrology went hand in hand. They believed celestial phenomena affected their earthly lives. Thus, they observed and documented Venus' risings for twenty-one years straight in the *Enuma Anu Enlil* tablets, along with the movements of other planets and principal stars. They knew when and where certain stars would appear just before sunrise (helical risings) and, stunningly, could predict when planets would come into alignment.

The Chaldean Neo-Babylonians chronicled the moon's phases and observed retrograde planet movement. (As the orbiting Earth passes other planets in their orbits, it appears some planets are moving backward). By 721 BCE, the Babylonians predicted and recorded lunar and solar eclipses; they thought eclipses were associated with a king's death or some other calamity. But their eclipse records have come in handy for today's historians to figure out when certain historical events occurred. They are also helpful for scientists analyzing the lunar orbit's long-term variations.

The Babylonian contribution to mathematics included the concepts of zero and place value. They counted by sixties rather than tens and could calculate reciprocal pairs equaling sixty when multiplied. As early as 1800 BCE, the Babylonians used algebra and fractions and solved cubic, linear, and quadratic equations. They could determine a circle's circumference and diameter, and a tablet dating to at least 1680 BCE showed they calculated pi (π) to a value of 3.125. Their understanding of trigonometry included using the Pythagorean theorem over a millennium before Pythagoras' birth, as recently discovered in 2021 through an analysis of the *Plimpton 322* tablet dating back to about 1800 BCE.[62]

Another brilliant contribution of the Babylonians was the *Code of Hammurabi,* a legal treatise written by the king in the eighteenth century BCE. Other law codes preceded his legal system, but Hammurabi's stood out for its detailed extensiveness. Its 282 laws covered legal issues related to marriage and family, commerce, wages, property, slavery, medical malpractice, and crimes including rape, theft, assault, incest, and kidnapping. His code even regulated barbers, construction workers, shipbuilders, doctors, and veterinarians in their trades. His stated purpose was "to prevent the strong from oppressing the weak and to see that justice is done to

[62] D. F. Mansfield, "Plimpton 322: A Study of Rectangles," *Foundations of Science* 26 (2021): 977-1005. https://doi.org/10.1007/s10699-021-09806-0

widows and orphans, so that I should enlighten the land, to further the well-being of mankind."

Hammurabi's Law Code (circa 1770 BCE) is etched into this black diorite pillar.
Hammurabi, CC BY 3.0 https://creativecommons.org/licenses/by/3.0 via Wikimedia Commons; https://commons.wikimedia.org/wiki/File:P1050763_Louvre_code_Hammurabi_face_rwk.JPG

Hammurabi had his law code carved into a finger-shaped stone pillar of black diorite more than seven feet high. Archaeologists discovered it 250 miles from Babylon in the Elamite capital of Susa, where the Elamites had taken it after raiding Babylon and stealing it. Moving the four-ton monument that far, presumably by oxcart, was a noteworthy feat! The hard diorite stone kept it well-preserved over the millennia. At the top is a carving of Hammurabi receiving the law from Shamash, god of the sun and justice. The rest of the monument has the 282 laws chiseled into its sides in cuneiform script.

Hammurabi harshly punished false accusations and false testimony with the death penalty; however, it was generally in the case of murder, adultery, or other crimes punishable by death. He also expected the judges to expend due diligence in determining guilt or innocence. If a judge carelessly gave a guilty verdict and collected a fine, and then later the defendant was proven innocent, the judge had to pay the defendant twelve times the fine and be permanently removed from the court.

Parts of *Hammurabi's Code* are strikingly similar to the *Law of Moses* written three centuries later in the *Torah*. For instance, the *Law of Moses* stated if someone hurt another person, the punishment must match the injury: a life for a life, an eye for an eye, and so on (Exodus 21). *Hammurabi's Code* said the same thing, except one could pay money in lieu of losing an eye or having one's teeth knocked out, and the amount of money depended on the social status of the injured person.

Moses and Hammurabi had similar civil laws, but *Hammurabi's Code* included many regulations regarding one's occupation, which the *Torah* did not. The *Torah* dealt a lot with religion: instructions on how to build the tabernacle, what the priests should wear, how to offer sacrifices, how to celebrate festivals, and warnings not to worship any other gods. Hammurabi's code barely mentioned religion, except stealing from temples, which got the death penalty.

Hammurabi's Code monument shows him standing before Shamash, the god of justice, and receiving the law.

Hammurabi's Law Code penalties were severe and heavy-handed, like cutting off an offender's hand, tongue, ear, or breast, or worse yet, execution. However, he led the way in legal views such as presuming innocence until proven guilty, determining whether an offender intended to cause harm, and considering mitigating circumstances influencing a crime. In these areas, he was a pioneer, as the Babylonians were in so many ways.

Chapter 10: Myths and Religion

Spirituality was paramount to the Babylonians, but what did they believe? What were their temples and festivals like, and how did they worship their gods? What do their myths tell us about their understanding of creation, the afterlife, and the character of their deities? This chapter will unpack the answers to these questions, exploring their macabre creation story and other captivating myths.

The Sumerians and Babylonians worshiped many of the same gods, but usually with different names. The *Enuma Elish* creation myth is about the younger gods staging a revolution, killing off the oldest gods, and establishing a new spiritual regime with Marduk as its head. The tale paralleled the reorganizing of religion when Babylon gained preeminence. The Sumerians had never worshipped Marduk, but Hammurabi elevated him from an obscure city god to Babylonia's supreme god, their nation's patron.

Ishtar (Inanna), the goddess of war and sexuality, remained popular in Babylonia, but a distant second to Marduk, although they did name the main gate of Babylon after her. Babylonian myths portrayed her in a somewhat unfavorable light; the *Epic of Gilgamesh* and *The Descent of Ishtar to the Underworld* (which we will dive into later in this chapter) characterize her as mercurial, spiteful, shameless, and grasping. She's not mentioned at all in the

Enuma Elish. The Babylonians tended to be more patriarchal and favored male gods.

Adad, the storm god, could send life-giving rain or deadly storms.
Drawn by Henri Faucher-Gudin after Austen Henry Layard, Public domain; https://commons.wikimedia.org/wiki/File:Ramman.png

According to the *Enuma Elish* myth, the Babylonians worshiped six hundred gods who answered to Marduk after he prevailed over Tiamat, the primordial goddess of chaos. Anu (An) was the Sumerian's chief god, and in Babylonia, he was Marduk's grandfather but less powerful than Marduk. One of Anu's sons, Adad, was originally a Semitic god (Hadad). The Babylonians worshiped Adad as the god of storms and portrayed him holding a lightning bolt or hammer, like the Greek Zeus or the Germanic Thor. The popular Sumerian god Enki (Ea) was Marduk's father, beloved by the Babylonians because he warned Utnapishtim to build the ark to save mankind and animals from the Great Flood. Ea was an auspicious god for incantations, magic, and exorcisms.

Babylon's most important temple was the Esagila, Marduk's sanctuary, but it also housed shrines to numerous other gods. Forty-three other temples stood in Babylon and fifty-five shrines of Marduk. Unlike the Assyrians and other nearby civilizations, the Babylonians constructed their imposing and exquisite architecture to please the gods rather than extol their military conquests.[63]

Festivities and worship connected the Babylonians with their gods, who erratically shifted from malevolence to kindheartedness. Failure to keep the gods contented through proper rituals could result in catastrophes like drought, disease, or military disaster. Thus, the priesthood and sorcerers organized worship ceremonies and festivals, fed the gods, adorned them with beautiful clothing and jewelry, chanted hymns and prayers, and offered sacrifices. Although Hammurabi ordered the death penalty for sorcery, by the Neo-Babylonian era, sorcerers were commonplace, needed to protect from evil spirits and interpret omens.

Religion and government were closely intertwined. The Babylonian New Year fell in the spring, in the month of Nissan, when it was time to cultivate the fields. Babylonians celebrated the New Year with the Akitu Festival, the year's most celebrated gala, lasting eleven days. An important ritual was the king taking the hand of Marduk's statue, giving legitimacy to the king and displaying Marduk's supremacy over the earthly monarchs.

At the beginning of the Akitu Festival, the priests carried the statue of Marduk and other gods in a grand parade. They marched down the Processional Way with its towering fifty-foot walls covered with gleaming, blue-glazed tiles featuring golden mosaics of lions, bulls, and dragons. Proceeding out the Ishtar Gate, the priests ceremoniously placed Marduk and his entourage of lesser gods in the Akitu temple, where they rested for the next few days.

---

[63] Andrew George, "Ancient Descriptions: The Babylonian Topographical Texts," in *Babylon*, ed. I. L. Finkel and M. J. Seymour. (New York: Oxford University Press, 2008), 161-5.

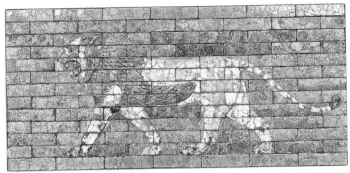

Mosaic lions adorned the blue-glazed bricks of the Processional Way.
https://commons.wikimedia.org/wiki/File:Passing_lion_Babylon_AO21118.jpg

The priests led the people in prayer for eleven days at the temples, telling the Enuma Elish creation story and acting out parts of it. The king would visit the Akitu Temple and strip off his royal robes, kneeling before Marduk and the other gods in humility. Marduk would mysteriously disappear on the seventh day, symbolizing he had left to fight Tiamat, goddess of chaos; his image would reappear the next day. On the tenth day, Marduk returned to the city with great pomp and dancing in the streets, blessing the upcoming planting season and ensuring the coming year's prosperity.

Marduk's presence within Babylon was critical to the city's well-being. If enemies stole his statue (which they did, repeatedly), Babylonians suffered calamities, as the Mesopotamians believed their gods inhabited the cult images. The *Marduk Prophecy* is a somewhat humorous account of Marduk's "travels" to Hatti, Assyria, and Elam, after enemies invaded and sacked Babylon, carrying Marduk off with their spoils of war.

Although Marduk couldn't resist capture or get himself back to Babylon without assistance, he actively participated in his travels. The narrative of the two tablets containing the *Marduk Prophecy* is in the first person; Marduk himself is telling the story. In it, Marduk describes his travels to Hatti and Assyria as if they were his idea and relates how the Hittites and Assyrians received him kindly.

The other gods followed Marduk to Elam on his third trip out of Babylon, leaving Babylon desolate. That trip wasn't as pleasant as the earlier ones; Marduk disliked his treatment by the Elamites. In the tablet found just behind the *Marduk Prophecy* tablet, known as the *Prophecy of Šulgi*, Marduk foretold that a brilliant new king of Babylon would trample Elam and rescue Marduk. The prophecy was likely propaganda written after the fact during Nebuchadnezzar I's reign, following his retrieval of Marduk.

The *Marduk Prophecy* doesn't list people's names or dates, but Marduk's journey to Hatti would have been in 1595 BCE when the Hittite king Mursili I laid waste to Babylon. He stole Marduk and ended the Amorite dynasty. The Kassites retrieved Marduk and ruled Babylon, but then the Assyrian king Tukulti-Ninurta I plundered Babylon, stealing Marduk again. The Assyrians themselves returned Marduk, fearing his retribution. Marduk's third "visit" was to Elam, after the Elamites conquered and ended the Kassite state in 1155 BCE.

The *Seven Tablets of Creation* (the *Enuma Elish*) was Babylonia's gruesome creation myth, explaining how Marduk gained preeminence over the other gods, created the earth and sky, appointed each of the six hundred gods to their duties, and oversaw the creation of humans. The oldest preserved tablets of the disturbing tale date back to about 1200 BCE, with notations that the scribes copied them from earlier tablets written before the Early Babylonian Era.

Although the story includes many Sumerian deities, Marduk rises above all the other gods as the grand champion over chaos. It begins as a bizarre retelling of the Sumerian *Eridu Genesis* (the Flood myth). In both tales, the oldest gods can't sleep because of the noisy youngsters. In the *Eridu Genesis,* the rambunctious humans keep the older gods awake, so the gods send the Great Flood. But Ea (Enki) intervenes and tells Utnapishtim to build the ark.

The god Enki (Ea) warned of the Great Flood.
Osama Shukir Muhammed Amin FRCP(Glasg), CC BY-SA 4.0
https://creativecommons.org/licenses/by-sa/4.0 via Wikimedia Commons;
https://commons.wikimedia.org/wiki/File:God_Ea_holding_a_cup._From_Nasiriyah,
_Iraq._2004-1595_BCE._Iraq_Museum.jpg

The *Enuma Elish* takes a different twist; it wasn't the humans being noisy, as they hadn't yet been created. It was the escapades of the unruly younger gods that were annoying the very first god Apsu (the begetter) and his wife Tiamat, goddess of chaos. Apsu represented fresh water, and Tiamat was the swirling, tumultuous ocean. When the two waters mingled, they created the other gods.

Almost immediately, Apsu and Tiamat regretted bringing the new life into being, as now they could not sleep with all the uproar from their children. But neither Apsu nor Tiamat reprimanded the younger gods for all their riotous dancing and clamor through the night. Finally, they couldn't bear it anymore, and they met to discuss the problem. Apsu declared: "Their behavior is infuriating! Night or day, I can't sleep! I'm going to kill them!"

"No!" Tiamat raged and wailed. "We can't murder our children. I know their behavior is deplorable, but can't we give them a chance? Let's scold them, punish their obnoxious behavior, and see if they will change."

Apsu's vizier Mummu interjected, "Father! Get rid of these rioters, and then you can sleep!"

Apsu grinned, happy that Mummu supported his plan to kill the unruly gods. Mummu curled up in Apsu's lap and kissed him. Tiamat fumed and cursed but could not persuade Apsu to let the young gods live. When the young gods heard that Apsu planned to kill them all, they were undone. Falling to the ground, they wailed in despair.

But the young god Enki, son of Anu, decided to act. Speaking an enchantment over Apsu, his magical powers put Apsu into a deep sleep. Overwrought, Mummu gasped but was powerless against Enki. Enki killed Apsu and, from his body, formed a house to live in: the Chamber of Destinies. He brought his bride Damkina into their magnificent new home, and they conceived a child, Marduk, who had four eyes, four ears, and fire exploding from his mouth. Anu gave his grandson Marduk the four winds: "Send them spinning and blowing, my child. Make a hurricane!"

Meanwhile, Tiamat was beside herself. She had tried to spare her offspring, but now they had killed her husband. Some of the gods were scolding her for letting it happen; she must retaliate! Tiamat joined forces with a new and powerful husband, Qingu. After Marduk's hurricane flooded her with a tidal wave, Tiamat conjured all her chaotic superpowers, producing new offspring with Qingu: eleven ghastly fanged demons with toxic blood and indomitable weapons. These fiendish creations would kill off the younger gods!

Enki approached his grandmother Tiamat, hoping to put her into an enchanted spell, as he'd done with Apsu. But Tiamat was ready for him, with earsplitting shrieks and incantations. Realizing he was outpowered, Enki stole away. Next, his father, Anu, tried to pacify Tiamat, but her spine-chilling screeches, sorceries, and demonic forces paralyzed Anu with fear. The rest of the gods bit their lips, powerless to do anything to defend themselves.

But then Marduk burst out in his chariot pulled by four mighty stallions: Trampler, Demolisher, Malevolent, and Speed. He summoned the seven winds to assault Tiamat's bowels. Qingu's witchcraft unnerved him, but he held his ground, raging at Tiamat, "You! Our mother! Why don't you defend your own children? Why do you despise us?"

But Tiamat was out of her mind with feverish fury, howling hexes and witchery as Marduk captured her in his battle net. He sent his hurricane into her gaping mouth, blowing up her body. Then he impaled her heart with his lance, crushed her skull, and eviscerated her. He captured and tied up Qingu, then trampled the eleven demons under his feet. Exhausted, Marduk sat down and inspected Tiamat's mangled body.

This bas-relief from Nineveh may depict the battle between Tiamat and Marduk.

His father Enki had made his house from Apsu's body, and Marduk would do the same with what was left of Tiamat! His new home would parallel Enki's. As one would filet a fish, Marduk split Tiamat into two halves, which became the sky and the earth. He formed the Euphrates and Tigris from the tears flowing out of her eyes. Marduk then created the moon and the stars to mark the passage of time and appointed the six hundred gods to their duties.

The gods gathered around their new leader with great applause, kissing his feet and acknowledging Marduk as their king. Marduk and Enki executed Qingu because he'd incited Tiamat to war against the gods. Enki used Qingu's blood to form the first man: Lullu. The humans would be useful in taking care of all the practical details of regular life so the gods could focus on running the universe.

The ecstatic gods cheered these new events and set to work building a stellar new city: Babylon. This magnificent place would be the home of Marduk and the chief gods. The gods built the Esagil temple for Marduk, then built temples for themselves. They happily sat down to a lavish feast when they finally finished all the construction, passing around the beer mugs and toasting their new king Marduk.

Another Babylonian myth, the *Epic of Erra*,[64] deals with Marduk's multiple "journeys" away from Babylon when he was "godnapped." Nergal (Erra), the god of war, was bored, so he decided to stir things up. It was no fun being the god of war when Babylonia was enjoying peace, and, for heaven's sake, he needed to ensure mankind would continue to worship him. "They hold me in contempt," he muttered repeatedly.

---

[64] Andrew George, "The Poem of Erra and Ishum: A Babylonian Poet's View of War," in *Warfare and Poetry in the Middle East*, ed. Hugh Kennedy (London: I. B. Tauris, 2013), 39-71.

Nergal used enchantments to trick Marduk into taking a trip away from Babylon, as his statue was in dire need of refurbishing. He promised Marduk he'd look after things in his absence. With Marduk gone, Nergal began implementing his plot to instigate war, but Marduk returned early, and Nergal had to put his plans on hold. Nergal bided his time, and eventually, Marduk left on another journey. Nergal took advantage of the chaos during Marduk's absence to stir up a horrific war in Nippur, receiving the praise of his vizier Ishum:

"Heaven's at your disposal, Hell's in your hands,

you have charge of Babylon; give orders to Esagil:

You're master of all the cosmic powers; even the gods are in terror of you...

is there warfare without you?"[65]

The war god Nergal almost destroyed the cosmic order in Marduk's absence.
https://commons.wikimedia.org/wiki/File:Illustrerad_Verldshistoria_band_I_Ill_034.jpg

---

[65] George, "The Poem of Erra," 54.

Gleefully feeding off the incomparable misery he caused by his indiscriminate violence and destruction, Nergal even made megalomaniac plans to upend the universe. He would unseat the cosmic government until every nation, city, family, and man annihilated each other. Aghast, his vizier Ishum created a distraction, launching a war on Mount Sharshar in Lebanon, the homeland of the fierce nomads that threatened Babylonia. Ishum flattened Mount Sharshar, felled the cedars of Lebanon, and created a tidal wave that swept over the land.

Ishum's violence somehow brought Nergal back to his senses. Nergal finally realized that if he destroyed all mankind, there would not be anyone to feed and serve the gods and take care of all the menial tasks that the gods created the humans to do:

"Without Ishum, my vanguard, what now would exist?

Where is your provisioner, where are your high priests?

Where are your food-offerings? You would smell no incense!"[66]

The Descent of Ishtar to the Underworld[67] is another bizarre Babylonian myth. Ishtar (Inanna), the goddess of sexuality and war, plotted a takeover of the underworld, where her sister Ereshkigal reigned as queen over the land of darkness. Ishtar arrived at the gate of the Land of No Return and rattled it. "Gatekeeper, ho! Open the gate! Let me enter! I'll break the lock, smash the door-posts, and force the gate open if you don't. Then I'll bring up the dead to eat the living!"

The gatekeeper called back, "Stop! Oh lady, do not destroy it! I will go and announce your name to my queen Ereshkigal."

---

[66] George, "The Poem of Erra," 59.

[67] "Descent of the Goddess Ishtar into the Lower World," in *The Civilization of Babylonia and Assyria*, Morris Jastrow, Jr. (1915). https://www.sacred-texts.com/ane/ishtar.htm

When the gatekeeper informed Queen Ereshkigal that her sister Ishtar had arrived, Ereshkigal trembled like a reed. "What has possessed her? Does she want to live here like me, eating clay as food and drinking dust as wine? Will she weep, like me, for the men here who are cut off from their families? For the wives torn from their husbands' embrace? For the little ones cut off before their time?"

"Go, gatekeeper, open the gate. Deal with her according to the ancient decree."

The gatekeeper passed up to the first gate, opening it. But as Ishtar passed through the gate, he removed her crown from her head. "Why did you remove my crown?" Ishtar asked.

"It is the ancient decree," the gatekeeper replied.

At the second gate, he removed her earrings. At the third, he removed her necklace. At the fourth, he removed her breast ornaments. At the fifth gate, he removed her girdle studded with semiprecious stones. At the sixth gate, he removed her bracelets and anklets. At the seventh and last gate, he removed her loincloth.

When Ishtar entered the Land of No Return, Ereshkigal bristled with anger when she saw her. Ishtar threw herself at Ereshkigal without a second thought, but Ereshkigal called to her vizier: "Namtar, throw her into the dungeon! Inflict her with sixty diseases as punishment: eye disease, heart disease, brain ailment; send disease against her entire body."

Meanwhile, in the Land of the Living, trouble was afoot. Ishtar was the goddess of sexuality; when she left the world, the bulls stopped mounting the cows, all the animals stopped mating, the men stopped approaching the young women in the street, and everyone slept alone. No animals or humans were reproducing. If this continued, all life would be gone! Shamash, the sun god, went weeping to Enki. With tears flowing, he told him that Ishtar had gone into the underworld, and all life would soon end.

Enki sent a messenger to the underworld, requesting that Ereshkigal release her sister and sprinkle her with the water of life. When Ereshkigal heard this, she bit her finger and cursed the messenger. "May the dregs from the city's gutters be your food! May the drunkards strike you on the cheek!"

Nevertheless, Ereshkigal obeyed Enki. She released Ishtar, sprinkled her with the water of life, then sent her out of the underworld, up through the seven gates. Ishtar retrieved her clothing and jewelry as she passed through the gates.

But for Ishtar to leave, someone had to replace her in the underworld. She looked up into the Land of the Living and saw her human husband, Tammuz, the shepherd. Instead of weeping for her, he was wearing festive garments and prancing about with his sister, playing a lapis lazuli flute! Indignant, Ishtar chose Tammuz to replace her in the underworld for six months of the year, and she returned for the other six months when the fields lay fallow.

While the Babylonian myths would probably give little children nightmares, they provide a fascinating insight into the Babylonian culture, beliefs, and values. They inform us about the Babylonian perception of cosmic order and the character of their deities. More than anything else, Babylon was a highly-respected religious center for Mesopotamia, a holy city. In the Babylonian mind, it was the center of the world.

Conclusion

The Babylonians sprang from humble origins as nomadic herders to build a stunningly beautiful city with up to 200,000 people at its peak, the largest city in the world for over two hundred years. They built massive city walls adorned with gleaming mosaics, elaborate temples, and a towering ziggurat that could be seen from twenty miles away. Their elegant hanging gardens were so impressive in beauty and engineering that the Greeks listed them as one of the seven wonders of the ancient world.

After the Assyrian Empire fell, the Neo-Babylonians rose to become the world's most powerful empire of the time, covering nearly 200,000 square miles with multiple ethnicities and languages. It encompassed modern-day Iraq, large swathes of Iran, Kuwait, Syria, Arabia, and Jordan, and stretched down the Mediterranean to include Lebanon, Israel, and Palestine. The multicultural milieu encouraged novel advances in the arts, architecture, and sciences.

The Babylonians were not monocultural; in Babylonia's three dominant eras, the Amorites first ruled, then the Kassites, and lastly, a mixture of Chaldeans and other ethnicities. In all three periods, Babylon was regarded as a holy city, the center of the world. Throughout its history, Babylon perpetuated the worship of

Marduk and a distinctive culture dedicated to exploring new knowledge about the universe, medicine, and mathematics.

What are our key takeaways from Babylonia's history? What lessons can we learn from its civilization and the events that shaped it into a nation? Awe-inspiring cultures had shaped Mesopotamia before the Babylonians rose to power: the Ubaid, the Sumerians, and the Akkadians. Master assimilators, the Babylonians borrowed freely from these previous cultures and their greatest rival, the Assyrians.

Through absorbing the knowledge, culture, and technologies of other civilizations, the cosmopolitan Babylonians helped preserve the ancient cultures while forging ahead with a blend of adaptability and innovation. When we learn from our own histories and the people and cultures around us, we remain relevant and adaptable, able to adjust to an ever-changing world and grow in creative energy and success.

To survive and thrive, the Babylonians had to build brilliant alliances with their neighbors and far-distant tribes. They even had to form alliances with their chief rival Assyria throughout their earlier history. These alliances were a definitive element in preserving their existence and eventually growing their empire to startling heights. Collaboration and cooperation often decide whether our endeavors succeed or fail, no matter what we hope to accomplish.

What are Babylonia's connections to modern society? How has this ancient civilization contributed to our global heritage? Where do we begin? The Babylonians gave us our seven-day week, four-week month, and twelve-month year. The Babylonian's astute studies of astronomy and their phenomenal breakthroughs in mathematics formed the underlying foundations of modern astrophysics, trigonometry, numerical analysis, and countless other applications in math and science. Today's medical science owes much to the Babylonians' development of diagnosis, medicines, surgical techniques, and wound care. Hammurabi's law code influenced our modern legal system's concepts of intent, mitigating circumstances affecting a crime, and presumption of innocence until proven guilty.

Babylon's revolutionary legacy lives on. We continue to benefit from Babylon's groundbreaking advances in so many areas of life. This exceptional and creative civilization still reaches through time to influence our everyday lives, even our calendars. Echoes of Babylon resound in our criminal justice system, scientific and mathematical understanding, art, architecture, and more. The city may have sunk into the sand over the past millennia, but its contributions to today's world persevere.

Here's another book by Enthralling History that you might like

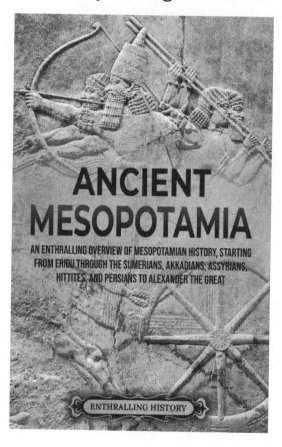

Free limited time bonus

Stop for a moment. We have a free bonus set up for you. The problem is this: we forget 90% of everything that we read after 7 days. Crazy fact, right? Here's the solution: we've created a printable, 1-page pdf summary for this book that you're reading now. All you have to do to get your free pdf summary is to go to the following website: **https://livetolearn.lpages.co/enthrallinghistory/**

Once you do, it will be intuitive. Enjoy, and thank you!

Bibliography

Assyrian King List. Livius. https://www.livius.org/sources/content/anet/564-566-the-assyrian-king-list/

Alstola, Tero. "Judean Merchants in Babylonia and Their Participation in Long-Distance Trade." *Die Welt Des Orients* 47, no. 1 (2017): 25–51. http://www.jstor.org/stable/26384887.

Beaulieu, Paul-Alain. *A History of Babylon, 2200 BC-AD 75.* Pondicherry: Wiley, 2018.

Beaulieu, Paul-Alain. *Reign of Nabonidus, King of Babylon (556-539 BC).* New Haven: Yale University Press, 1989.

Bertman, Stephen. *Handbook to Life in Ancient Mesopotamia.* Oxford: Oxford University Press, 2005.

Boivin, Odette. *The First Dynasty of the Sealand in Mesopotamia.* Volume 20: Studies in Ancient Near Eastern Records. Boston: De Gruyter, 2018.

Broad, William J. "It Swallowed a Civilization." *New York Times,* October 21, 2003. https://www.nytimes.com/2003/10/21/science/it-swallowed-a-civilization.html

Carter, R., and Graham Philip, eds. *Beyond the Ubaid: Transformation and Integration in the Late Prehistoric Societies of the Middle East.* Chicago: The Oriental Institute, University of Chicago, 2010.

Chavalas, M. W., ed. *The Ancient Near East: Historical Sources in Translation.* Malden, MA: Blackwell Publishing, 2006.

Chronicle of Early Kings (ABC 20). Livius. https://www.livius.org/sources/content/mesopotamian-chronicles-content/abc-20-chronicle-of-early-kings

Cserkits, Michael. "The Concept of War in Ancient Mesopotamia: Reshaping Carl von Clausewitz's Trinity." *Expeditions with MCUP,* United States Marine Corps University Press, 2022. https://doi.org/10.36304/ExpwMCUP.2022.01

Cuneiform Texts from Babylonian Tablets in the British Museum: Part XIII. Piccadilly: Longmans and Co., 1901.

Dalley, Stephanie. *Myths from Mesopotamia Creation, the Flood, Gilgamesh, and Others.* Oxford: Oxford University Press, 2008.

Da Riva, Rocío. "The Figure of Nabopolassar in Late Achaemenid and Hellenistic Historiographic Tradition: BM 34793 and CUA 90." *Journal of Near Eastern Studies* 76, no.1. https://www.journals.uchicago.edu/doi/full/10.1086/690464

Deams, A. and K. Croucher. "Artificial Cranial Modification in Prehistoric Iran: Evidence from Crania and Figurines." *Iranica Antiqua* 42 (2007):1-21.

De Boer, Rients. "Beginnings of Old Babylonian Babylon: Sumu-Abum and Sumu-La-El." *Free University of Amsterdam.* American Schools of Oriental Research. https://www.jstor.org/journal/jcunestud

De Graef, Katrien. "Dual Power in Susa: Chronicle of a Transitional Period from Ur III via Šimaški to the Sukkalmaḥs." *Bulletin of the School of Oriental and African Studies,* University of

London 75, no. 3 (2012): 525–46.
http://www.jstor.org/stable/41811207.

"Descent of the Goddess Ishtar into the Lower World." In *The Civilization of Babylonia and Assyria*, Morris Jastrow, Jr., 1915. https://www.sacred-texts.com/ane/ishtar.htm

Editors. "The World's Oldest Writing." *Archaeology*, May/June 2016. https://www.archaeology.org/issues/213-features/4326-cuneiform-the-world-s-oldest-writing

Enthralling History. *Ancient Mesopotamia: An Enthralling Overview of Mesopotamian History,*

Starting from Eridu through the Sumerians, Akkadian Empire, Assyrians, Hittites, and Persians to Alexander the Great. Coppell, Texas: Joelan AB, 2022.

Enthralling History. *The Akkadian Empire: An Enthralling Overview of the Rise and Fall of the Akkadians.* Coppell, Texas: Joelan AB, 2022.

Finkel, Irving. "The Lament of Nabû-šuma-ukîn." In *Focus Mesopotamischer Geschichte, Wiege früher Gelehrtsamkeit, Mythos in der Moderne.* Saaerbrücken, 1999.

George, Andrew. "Ancient Descriptions: The Babylonian Topographical Texts." In *Babylon*, edited by I. L. Finkel and M. J. Seymour. New York: Oxford University Press, 2008, 161-165.

George, Andrew. "The Poem of Erra and Ishum: A Babylonian Poet's View of War." In *Warfare and Poetry in the Middle East,* edited by Hugh Kennedy, 39-71. London: I. B. Tauris, 2013.

George, Andrew. "The Tower of Babel: Archaeology, History and Cuneiform Texts." *Archiv für Orientforschung,* 51 (2005/2006): 75–95.

https://eprints.soas.ac.uk/3858/2/TowerOfBabel.AfO.pdf

Grayson, A. K. *Babylonian Historical-Literary Texts: Toronto Semitic Texts and Studies, 3*. Toronto: University of Toronto Press, 1975.

Herodotus. *Capture of Babylon*. Livius. https://www.livius.org/articles/person/darius-the-great/sources/capture-of-babylon-herodotus

Hritz, Carrie, Jennifer Pournelle, Jennifer Smith, and سميث‌جنيفر. "Revisiting the Sealands: Report of Preliminary Ground Reconnaissance in the Hammar District, Dhi Qar and Basra Governorates, Iraq." *Iraq* 74 (2012): 37–49. http://www.jstor.org/stable/23349778.

Huber, Peter J. *Astronomical Dating of Babylon I and Ur III*. Cambridge: Harvard University, 1982.

Jacobsen, Thorkild. "The Assumed Conflict between Sumerians and Semites in Early Mesopotamian History." *Journal of the American Oriental Society* 59, no. 4 (1939): 485–95. https://doi.org/10.2307/594482.

Jastrow, Jr., Morris. "Did the Babylonian Temples Have Libraries?" *Journal of the American Oriental Society* 27 (1906): 147-182. https://www.jstor.org/stable/pdf/592857.pdf

Jones, Tom B. "By the Rivers of Babylon Sat We Down." *Agricultural History* 25, no. 1 (1951): 1–9. http://www.jstor.org/stable/3740293.

Kerrigan, Michael. *The Ancients in Their Own Words*. London: Amber Books, 2019.

King, Leonard W. *A History of Sumer and Akkad: An Account of the Early Races of Babylonia from Prehistoric Times to the Foundation of the Babylonian Monarchy*. New York: Amulet Press, 2015 (first published 1910).

Koppen, Frans van. "The Old to Middle Babylonian Transition: History and Chronology of the Mesopotamian Dark Age." *Ägypten Und Levante / Egypt and the Levant* 20 (2010): 453–63. http://www.jstor.org/stable/23789952

Lawrence, D., A. Palmisano, and M. W. de Gruchy. "Collapse and Continuity: A Multi-proxy Reconstruction of Settlement Organization and Population Trajectories in the Northern Fertile Crescent during the 4.2kya Rapid Climate Change Event." *PLoS One.* 16 (1) (2021). https://pubmed.ncbi.nlm.nih.gov/33428648

Leemans, W. F. "The Trade Relations of Babylonia and the Question of Relations with Egypt in the Old Babylonian Period." *Journal of the Economic and Social History of the Orient 3*, no. 1 (1960): 21–37. https://doi.org/10.2307/3596027

Levin, Yigal. "Nimrod the Mighty, King of Kish, King of Sumer and Akkad." *Vetus Testamentum 52*, no. 3 (2002): 350–66. http://www.jstor.org/stable/1585058.

Lambert, W. G. "Studies in Marduk." *Bulletin of the School of Oriental and African Studies, University of London 47*, no. 1 (1984): 1–9. http://www.jstor.org/stable/618314.

Mansfield, D.F. "Plimpton 322: A Study of Rectangles." *Foundations of Science 26* (2021): 977–1005. https://doi.org/10.1007/s10699-021-09806-0

Mark, Joshua J. "Ashurnasirpal II." *World History Encyclopedia.* https://www.worldhistory.org/Ashurnasirpal_II

Mark, Joshua J. "The Marduk Prophecy." *World History Encyclopedia.* 2016. https://www.worldhistory.org/article/990/the-marduk-prophecy

Marriage of Martu. The Electronic Text Corpus of Sumerian Literature. Oxford: University of Oxford. https://etcsl.orinst.ox.ac.uk/section1/tr171.htm

Moore, A. M. T. "Pottery Kiln Sites at al' Ubaid and Eridu." *Iraq* 64 (2002): 69–77. https://doi.org/10.2307/4200519

Nemet-Nejat, Karen Rhea. *Daily Life in Ancient Mesopotamia.* Westport, Connecticut: Greenwood Press, 1998.

Prayer of Nabonidus (4Q242). Livius. https://www.livius.org/sources/content/dss/4q242-prayer-of-nabonidus

Sackrider, Scott. "The History of Astronomy in Ancient Mesopotamia." *The NEKAAL Observer* 234. https://nekaal.org/observer/ar/ObserverArticle234.pdf

Stol, Marten. "Women in Mesopotamia." *Journal of the Economic and Social History of the Orient* 38, no. 2 (1995): 123–44. http://www.jstor.org/stable/3632512

Sumerian King List. Translated by Jean-Vincent Scheil, Stephen Langdon, and Thorkild Jacobsen. Livius. https://www.livius.org/sources/content/anet/266-the-sumerian-king-list/#Translation

Teall, Emily K. "Medicine and Doctoring in Ancient Mesopotamia." *Grand Valley Journal of History* 3:1 (2014), Article 2. https://scholarworks.gvsu.edu/gvjh/vol3/iss1/2

The Chronicle Concerning the Reign of Nabonidus (ABC 7). Livius, 2020. https://www.livius.org/sources/content/mesopotamian-chronicles-content/abc-7-nabonidus-chronicle

The Chronicle Concerning Year Three of Neriglissar (ABC 6). Livius, 2006. https://www.livius.org/sources/content/mesopotamian-chronicles-content/abc-6-neriglissar-chronicle

The Code of Hammurabi. Translated by L.W. King. The Avalon Project: Documents in Law, History, and Diplomacy. Yale Law School: Lillian Goldman Law Library. https://avalon.law.yale.edu/ancient/hamframe.asp

The Epic of Atrahasis. Translated by B. R. Foster. Livius.

https://www.livius.org/sources/content/anet/104-106-the-epic-of-atrahasis

The Tanakh: Full Text. Jewish Virtual Library: A Project of AICE. 1997. https://www.jewishvirtuallibrary.org/the-tanakh-full-text

The Tummal Chronicle. Livius. https://www.livius.org/sources/content/mesopotamian-chronicles-content/cm-7-tummal-chronicle

Van De Mieroop, Marc. *A History of the Ancient Near East ca. 3000 - 323 BC.* Hoboken: Blackwell Publishing, 2006.

Van De Mieroop, Marc. *King Hammurabi of Babylon: A Biography.* Hoboken: Blackwell Publishing, 2005.

Verse Account of Nabonidus. Translated by A. Leo Oppenheim. Livius. https://www.livius.org/sources/content/anet/verse-account-of-nabonidus

Vlaardingerbroek, Menko. "The Founding of Nineveh and Babylon in Greek Historiography." *Iraq* 66 (2004): 233–41. https://doi.org/10.2307/4200577.

Weiershäuser, Frauke, and Jamie Novotny. *The Royal Inscriptions of Amēl-Marduk (561–560 BC), Neriglissar (559–556 BC), and Nabonidus (555–539 BC), Kings of Babylon* (PDF). Winona Lake: Eisenbrauns, 2020.

Weidner Chronicle (ABC 19). Livius, 2020. https://www.livius.org/sources/content/mesopotamian-chronicles-content/abc-19-weidner-chronicle

Weiss, Harvey. *Megadrought and Collapse.* New York: Oxford University Press, 2017.

Weiss, H., M. A. Courty, W. Wetterstrom, F. Guichard, L. Senior, R. Meadow, and A. Curnow. "The Genesis and Collapse of Third Millennium North Mesopotamian Civilization." *Science* 261, no. 5124 (1993): 995–1004. http://www.jstor.org/stable/2881847.

Woolley, C. Leonard. "Excavations at Ur." *Journal of the Royal Society of Arts* 82, no. 4227 (1933): 46–59. http://www.jstor.org/stable/41360003.

Year Names of Ibbi-Suen. CDLI Wiki. University of Oxford. *https://cdli.ox.ac.uk/wiki/doku.php?id=year_names_ibbi-suen*

Xenophon. *Cyropaedia: The Education of Cyrus.* Translated by Henry Graham Dakyns. Project Gutenberg EBook. https://www.gutenberg.org/files/2085/2085-h/2085-h.htm

Made in the USA
Columbia, SC
17 October 2024

44495342R00087